T0375643

Words and Works of Jesus

Aloysius Aseervatham

WESTBOW
PRESS®
A DIVISION OF THOMAS NELSON
& ZONDERVAN

WestBow Press books may be ordered through booksellers or by contacting:

WestBow Press
A Division of Thomas Nelson & Zondervan
1663 Liberty Drive
Bloomington, IN 47403
www.westbowpress.com
1 (866) 928-1240

Scripture taken from the King James Version of the Bible.

ISBN: 978-1-9736-5532-9 (sc)
ISBN: 978-1-9736-5534-3 (hc)
ISBN: 978-1-9736-5533-6 (e)

Library of Congress Control Number: 2019902371

Print information available on the last page.

WestBow Press rev. date: 3/7/2019

Contents

Table of Parables

Table of Miracles

Preface

In 1969 my father, who was an author, printer and publisher, released a book titled "HOLY WORDS OF JESUS" in Tamil, a language indigenous to Sri Lanka and Southern India. His ambition at the time was to get his work translated into English. After 39 years, I was able to fulfil his ambition by releasing the translation to all interested persons. I thank and praise the Holy Spirit for providing me the interest and the courage to take on this complex task.

I am now republishing the translation under the title "WORDS AND WORKS OF JESUS. The subject matter of the book is essentially the teachings or the words of Jesus, but I have now added some Old Testament stories and Crossword Puzzles. This enhances the book's value as a resource for educational purposes to parents and all other interested persons.

The purpose of this book is twofold; firstly, to present a large volume of material in the Bible relevant to modern living in a form that can be easily absorbed and secondly to provide an insight into the 'Good news' to interested non-Christians. Although there are numerous books of this type in the market, I am hopeful that the logical presentation of this book and its simplicity will provide enlightenment and understanding.

I firmly believe that anyone with a sound knowledge of the eternal words of the Great Teacher - Jesus, the Son of God - will contribute enormously to the peace and harmony of the troubled world we live in. All problems, worries, anger, and guilt can be dealt with through simple faith in Jesus' Words.

Aloysius Aseervatham
February 2019

Foreword

High up in the Himalaya's in the country of Bhutan there is a sign "Let there be peace on Earth". Peace is the gift which every human being seeks. Even the most violent of perpetrators believe that through their actions they will obtain the peace they desire for themselves and others.

Our world is, in one sense, becoming smaller. Cultures and religions which seemed far away are now present in our communities through the migration of people seeking better life. With this interaction between peoples of various countries, religions and cultures, it is important as we seek peace, that we endeavor to understand the religious beliefs of others.

The human heart is meant to love and to nourish peace. Jesus Christ the great teacher taught that to attain peace: Love your enemies, do good to them which hate you." (Luke 6: 27 KJV)

Christianity has had enormous influence on the lives of people of many cultures and races for over 2 000 years. This book will help Christians to deepen their knowledge and faith in Jesus Christ. For the non-Christians it will impart knowledge of the life and teaching of Jesus Christ.

Aloysius Aseervatham's father will be very happy that his son has fulfilled his wishes by publishing his work in English. May all who read and savor this book come to know that that there is hope and promise of peace for the human family when we endeavor to build bridges of trust and understanding among peoples of various cultures and religions.

Daniel Carroll

Parish Priest
Darra — Jindalee, Queensland
Australia

Dedication

This book is dedicated to two important people in my life whose love, affection, advice and support I was privileged to receive for a long time. One is my loving father, M.V. Aseervatham, and the other is my beloved wife, Jasmine Aseervatham.

Acknowledgement

Several people, friends, and relatives helped me in writing this book with their valuable individual input. I am very grateful to them. I thank my grandsons, Joshua and Nicholas, for their assistance in formatting and reviewing this book.

If the life changing messages in "words and works of Jesus" have an impact on the lives of people, I would have truly succeeded in facilitating my father's vision when he wrote his original book.

I praise and thank GOD for making this service a part of his will for my life

AA

People of Judaea

Judaea is also known as Judea or Judah. It is a territory in Southwest Asia and a region of historic Palestine. Its boundaries include Jerusalem in the North, the Jordan River and the Dead Sea in the East, the coast of Mediterranean Sea in the west and a Southern border near Negev desert.

The three major religious societies in Judaea at the time of Jesus were the Pharisees, the Sadducees, and the Essenes. The Pharisees were often the most vocal, influential and loyal to God. They were the most bitter, and deadly opponents of Jesus and His message. They became blind to the Messiah when He was in their very midst. They saw His miracles and they heard His Words, but instead of receiving him with joy, they did all that they could to stop Him - eventually to the point of getting Him killed when He truthfully claimed to be the Son of God.

The Sadducees were a priestly and aristocratic group, who opposed the Pharisees' use of Oral Law and also differed with the Pharisees on many theological tenets. They tended to disassociate God from human affairs. They played a leading role in the trial and condemnation of Jesus.

The Essenes are a group that literally abandoned Jerusalem, it seems, in protest to the way the Temple was being run. This was a group that went out in the desert to prepare the way of the Lord, following the commands, as they saw it, of the prophet Isaiah.

The Scribes, denoted by their blue robes, was scholarly and studious. They performed many tasks but were often specialists. They were the second of the High Castes. In Jesus' period the scribes were the professional interpreters of the Law in the Jewish synagogues.

Gentiles were simply non-Israelites, not from the stock of Abraham. The Samaritans are not a Jewish people, but rather a mix of several different peoples that worshipped various gods.

Chapter 1
The Good News

Before looking at the teachings of Jesus, it is appropriate to have some understanding of the structure and content of the Bible, namely the Old Testament and the New Testament.

Learning Outcome

- know the definition of the word *'Bible'*
- know what the Old Testament and the New Testament are
- know the four authors of the gospels

The Bible

The Bible is a collection of writings held to be of divine and human origin or a record of the relevant events in history relating to God's intervention with humanity. It is a complex collection of historical facts and a variety of other forms of information (parables, sermons, psalms and so on)

The word 'Bible' (derived from the Greek words *ta biblia*) means "revelation of God's words." It is also referred to as the holy scripture. The Bible has been translated into major languages of the world. More than forty persons were used as instruments by God in writing the Bible.

The Bible contains two major sections, namely the Old Testament and the New Testament. The Old Testament (the old covenant between God and Israel) begins with God's creation of the universe and continues by describing the mighty acts of God in and through his people. The New Testament (a new covenant for all) describes the life and ministry of Jesus and the growth of the early Christian community. In this book, we focus our attention mainly on the gospels, which are the four accounts at the beginning of the New Testament about the saving work of God in his son, Jesus Christ. Some Old Testament characters and their stories are just briefly mentioned, and a complete knowledge of the Old Testament could be gained by reading the many available resources.

The Four Gospels of the New Testament

The gospels were written by four authors: Matthew, Mark, Luke, and John. Some believe that these were written in that order. Not all scholars agree on the order of the writings, but the order is irrelevant!

St. Matthew

St. Matthew was the son of Alpheus from Galilee, from the clan of Levite. Jesus summoned Matthew to follow him while he was working as a tax collector for the Roman Empire in Capernaum. In the forty-first year after Christ, he wrote the gospel in Hebrew for the benefit of the Jews. Later it was translated by others into Greek. He died as a martyr at the hands of pagans in Ethiopia.

St. Mark

St. Mark was St. Peter's disciple. After St. Peter established the church in Rome, in accordance with the wishes of the people, St. Mark wrote the gospel preached by St. Peter in Greek approximately forty-five years after Christ. The good news written by St. Mark is believed to have been available in Latin as well.

St. Mark was sent as the bishop of the capital city of Egypt, where he spent many years struggling to establish the church. In the year AD 64, when he was en route to the cathedral of Alexandria, people who were jealous of seeing him convert thousands to Christianity tied a rope around his neck, dragged him over rocks, and killed him. He thus died as a martyr.

St. Luke

St. Luke was a companion of St. Paul while Paul was preaching in Antioch, the capital of Syria. St. Luke excelled in art and medicine.

He wrote the gospel in Greek for the benefit of the societies established by St. John. He also wrote the Acts of the Apostles. He died at the age of eighty-four.

St. John

St. John was one of Jesus's first twelve disciples. He was the son of Zebedee and the brother of James. St. John was the only disciple near the foot of the cross when Jesus was crucified. He was very much loved by Jesus and was charged with the responsibility of looking after Mary, the mother of Jesus.

St. John wrote the gospel in Greek. Because he wrote the gospel last, instead of any repetition, he only concentrated on writing the main events in Jesus's life.

Focus Questions

1	What is the meaning of the word "Bible?	5	What is the Old Testament?
2	By what another name is the Bible known?	6	What is the New Testament?
3	How many authors wrote the Bible?	7	What are gospels?
4	How many sections are contained in the Bible?	8	Who are the four authors of the gospels?

Note:

The complexity of the Bible is a consequence of many factors, such as the combination of several versions of historical events, the collation of passages with similar aims or concepts (psalms, proverbs, and prophecies), and the addition of information through the ages. The result is a comprehensive collection of information relating to the core beliefs of Judaism and Christianity, but it is difficult to grasp in its entirety—hence, the centuries of discussion and disagreement regarding the interpretation of every part of the Bible. Believers would argue that this is because the Bible was written by men inspired by God, and inevitably it will not be easy for the ordinary people to understand the divinity of God and his power.

It is important, therefore, to ponder the scriptures with spiritual focus, experiencing the Holy Spirit and reorienting our perspectives so that we can see through God's eyes and understand the hidden messages instead of reading them just for the *raw data* they provide.

Reflection

Over the last few decades, there has been a noticeable change in the acceptance of, and reliance on, the Bible as a source of guidance. The relevance of the Bible's messages in today's society are increasingly questioned; however, the ethical stance adopted by the Bible thousands of years ago is still relevant today. If we begin by viewing the Bible as a series of teachings on ethics and morals, its relevance today is apparent. If we add to this the power of faith in its teachings, its value as a spiritual assembly point for humanity marks the Bible as one of the most important books in the world.

Chapter 2
Births of John and Jesus

John the Baptist was born to be the forerunner of Jesus. He and Jesus were cousins and were born six months apart. John's birth is celebrated on June 24, and Jesus's is celebrated on December 25. The details associated with their births are considered in this chapter.

Learning Outcome

- know how John the Baptist was born
- know how Jesus was born
- know the events in Jesus's life soon after he was born

Announcement of the Birth of John the Baptist

There was in the days of Herod, the king of Judaea, a certain priest named Zacharias, of the course of Abia: and his wife was of the daughters of Aaron, and her name was Elisabeth. And they were both righteous before God, walking in all the commandments and ordinances of the Lord blameless.

And they had no child, because that Elisabeth was barren, and they both were now well stricken in years.

And it came to pass, that while he executed the priest's office before God in the order of his course,

According to the custom of the priest's office, his lot was to burn incense when he went into the temple of the Lord.

5

And the whole multitude of the people were praying without at the time of incense.

And there appeared unto him an angel of the Lord standing on the right side of the altar of incense.

And when Zacharias saw him, he was troubled, and fear fell upon him.

But the angel said unto him, Fear not, Zacharias: for thy prayer is heard; and thy wife Elisabeth shall bear thee a son, and thou shalt call his name John.

And thou shalt have joy and gladness; and many shall rejoice at his birth.

For he shall be great in the sight of the Lord and shall drink neither wine nor strong drink; and he shall be filled with the Holy Ghost, even from his mother's womb.

And many of the children of Israel shall he turn to the Lord their God.

And he shall go before him in the spirit and power of Elias, to turn the hearts of the fathers to the children, and the disobedient to the wisdom of the just; to make ready a people prepared for the Lord. (Luke 1:5–17 KJV)

Zacharias said to the angel, "Whereby shall I know this? for I am an old man, and my wife well stricken in years" (Luke 1:18 KJV).

The angel answered,

I am Gabriel, that stand in the presence of God; and am sent to speak unto thee, and to shew thee these glad tidings.

And, behold, thou shalt be dumb, and not able to speak, until the day that these things shall be performed, because thou believest not my words, which shall be fulfilled in their season. (Luke 1:19–20 KJV)

Announcement of the Birth of Jesus

And in the sixth month the angel Gabriel was sent from God unto a city of Galilee, named Nazareth,

To a virgin espoused to a man whose name was Joseph, of the house of David; and the virgin's name was Mary.

And the angel came in unto her, and said, Hail, thou that art highly favored, the Lord is with thee: blessed art thou among women.

And when she saw him, she was troubled at his saying, and cast in her mind what manner of salutation this should be.

And the angel said unto her, Fear not, Mary: for thou hast found favor with God.

And, behold, thou shalt conceive in thy womb, and bring forth a son, and shalt call his name Jesus. (Luke 1:26–31 KJV)

Mary said to the angel,

How shall this be, seeing I know not a man?

And the angel answered and said unto her, The Holy Ghost shall come upon thee, and the power of the Highest shall overshadow thee: therefore, also that holy thing which shall be born of thee shall be called the Son of God.

And, behold, thy cousin Elisabeth, she hath also conceived a son in her old age: and this is the sixth month with her, who was called barren.

For with God nothing shall be impossible.

And Mary said, Behold the handmaid of the Lord; be it unto me according to thy word. And the angel departed from her. (Luke 1:34-38 KJV)

Mary Visits Elizabeth

And Mary arose in those days, and went into the hill country with haste, into a city of Juda;

And entered into the house of Zacharias, and saluted Elisabeth.

And it came to pass, that, when Elisabeth heard the salutation of Mary, the babe leaped in her womb; and Elisabeth was filled with the Holy Ghost:

And she spoke out with a loud voice, and said, Blessed art thou among women, and blessed is the fruit of thy womb.

And whence is this to me, that the mother of my Lord should come to me?

For, lo, as soon as the voice of thy salutation sounded in mine ears, the babe leaped in my womb for joy.
(Luke 1: 39-44 KJV)

The Birth of John the Baptist

And Mary abode with her about three months and returned to her own house.
(Luke 1: 56 KJV)

Now Elisabeth's full time came that she should be delivered; and she brought forth a son.

And her neighbors and her cousins heard how the Lord had shewed great mercy upon her; and they rejoiced with her.

And it came to pass, that on the eighth day they came to circumcise the child; and they called him Zacharias, after the name of his father.

And his mother answered and said, Not so; but he shall be called John.

And they said unto her, there is none of thy kindred that is called by this name.

And they made signs to his father, how he would have him called.

And he asked for a writing table, and wrote, saying, His name is John. And they marveled all.

And his mouth was opened immediately, and his tongue loosed, and he spoke, and praised God.
(Luke 1: 57-64 KJV)

The Birth of Jesus Christ

Now the birth of Jesus Christ was on this wise: When as his mother Mary was espoused to Joseph, before they came together, she was found with child of the Holy Ghost.

Then Joseph her husband, being a just man, and not willing to make her a public example, was minded to put her away privily.

But while he thought on these things, behold, the angel of the Lord appeared unto him in a dream, saying, Joseph, thou son of David, fear not to take unto thee Mary thy wife: for that which is conceived in her is of the Holy Ghost.

And she shall bring forth a son, and thou shalt call his name Jesus: for he shall save his people from their sins.

Now all this was done, that it might be fulfilled which was spoken of the Lord by the prophet, saying,

Behold, a virgin shall be with child, and shall bring forth a son, and they shall call his name Emmanuel, which being interpreted is, God with us.

Then Joseph being raised from sleep did as the angel of the Lord had bidden him, and took unto him his wife:

And knew her not till she had brought forth her firstborn son: and he called his name Jesus.
(Matthew 1: 18-25 KJV)

Events Connected with the Birth of Jesus

Census and Birth of Jesus

And it came to pass in those days, that there went out a decree from Caesar Augustus that all the world should be taxed.
(And this taxing was first made when Cyrenius was governor of Syria.)

And all went to be taxed, everyone into his own city.

And Joseph also went up from Galilee, out of the city of Nazareth, into Judaea, unto the city of David, which is called Bethlehem; (because he was of the house and lineage of David:)

To be taxed with Mary his espoused wife, being great with child.

And so it was, that, while they were there, the days were accomplished that she should be delivered.

And she brought forth her firstborn son, and wrapped him in swaddling clothes, and laid him in a manger; because there was no room for them in the inn.
(Luke 2: 1-7 KJV)

Shepherds and the Angels

And there were in the same country shepherds abiding in the field, keeping watch over their flock by night.

And, lo, the angel of the Lord came upon them, and the glory of the Lord shone round about them: and they were sore afraid.

And the angel said unto them, Fear not: for, behold, I bring you good tidings of great joy, which shall be to all people.

. For unto you is born this day in the city of David a Saviour, which is Christ the Lord.

And this shall be a sign unto you; Ye shall find the babe wrapped in swaddling clothes, lying in a manger.

And suddenly there was with the angel a multitude of the heavenly host praising God, and saying,

Glory to God in the highest, and on earth peace, good will toward men.

And it came to pass, as the angels were gone away from them into heaven, the shepherds said one to another, Let us now go even unto Bethlehem, and see this thing which is come to pass, which the Lord hath made known unto us.

And they came with haste, and found Mary, and Joseph, and the babe lying in a manger.
(Luke 2: 8-16 KJV)

Visitors from the East

Now when Jesus was born in Bethlehem of Judaea in the days of Herod the king, behold, there came wise men from the east to Jerusalem,

Saying, where is he that is born King of the Jews? for we have seen his star in the east and are come to worship him.

When Herod the king had heard these things, he was troubled, and all Jerusalem with him.

And when he had gathered all the chief priests and scribes of the people together, he demanded of them where Christ should be born.

And they said unto him, In Bethlehem of Judaea: for thus it is written by the prophet,

And thou Bethlehem, in the land of Juda, art not the least among the princes of Juda: for out of thee shall come a Governor, that shall rule my people Israel.

Then Herod, when he had privily called the wise men, enquired of them diligently what time the star appeared.

And he sent them to Bethlehem, and said, Go and search diligently for the young child; and when ye have found him, bring me word again, that I may come and worship him also.

When they had heard the king, they departed; and, lo, the star, which they saw in the east, went before them, till it came and stood over where the young child was.

When they saw the star, they rejoiced with exceeding great joy.

And when they were come into the house, they saw the young child with Mary his mother, and fell down, and worshipped him: and when they had opened their treasures, they presented unto him gifts; gold, and frankincense and myrrh.

And being warned of God in a dream that they should not return to Herod, they departed into their own country another way.
(Matthew 2: 1-12 KJV)

Naming of Jesus

And when eight days were accomplished for the circumcising of the child, his name was called Jesus, which was so named of the angel before he was conceived in the womb.
(Luke 2: 21 KJV)

Jesus is also called Christ. Christ means "the anointed one."

Jesus is Presented in the Temple

And when the days of her purification according to the law of Moses were accomplished, they brought him to Jerusalem, to present him to the Lord; (As it is written in the law of the Lord, every male that openeth the womb shall be called holy to the Lord;)

And to offer a sacrifice according to that which is said in the law of the Lord, A pair of turtledoves, or two young pigeons.
(Luke 2: 22-24 KJV)

The Escape to Egypt

Behold, the angel of the Lord appeared to Joseph in a dream, saying, Arise, and take the young child and his mother, and flee into Egypt, and be thou there until I bring thee word: for Herod will seek the young child to destroy him.

When he arose, he took the young child and his mother by night, and departed into Egypt:

And was there until the death of Herod: that it might be fulfilled which was spoken of the Lord by the prophet, saying, Out of Egypt have I called my son.
(Matthew 2: 13-15 KJV)

The killing of the Children

Then Herod, when he saw that he was mocked of the wise men, was exceeding wroth, and sent forth, and slew all the children that were in Bethlehem, and in all the coasts thereof, from two years old and under, according to the time which he had diligently inquired of the wise men.
(Matthew 2: 16 KJV)

The Return from Egypt

But when Herod was dead, behold, an angel of the Lord appeared in a dream to Joseph in Egypt,

Saying, Arise, and take the young child and his mother, and go into the land of Israel: for they are dead which sought the young child's life.

And he arose, and took the young child and his mother, and came into the land of Israel.

But when he heard that Archelaus did reign in Judaea in the room of his father Herod, he was afraid to go thither: notwithstanding, being warned of God in a dream, he turned aside into the parts of Galilee:

And he came and dwelt in a city called Nazareth: that it might be fulfilled which was spoken by the prophets, He shall be called a Nazarene. (Matthew 2: 19-23 KJV)

Focus Questions

1	Who was the Ruler of Judea at the time of birth of John the Baptist?	5	Which town in Judaea was Jesus born?
2	Who are the parents of John the Baptist?	6	Who was the king of Judaea at the time of Jesus' birth?]
3	What happened to Zacharias when he refused to believe the angel about his wife becoming pregnant?	7	Where did Joseph and Mary flee to with Jesus when Herod was plotting to kill him?
4	What was special about the way Jesus was conceived by Mary?	8	Where did Jesus live during his early years?

Note:

The events surrounding the births of John the Baptist and Jesus give us an idea of the way God influences our lives. Is it possible that we have lost the ability to recognize messages and help sent to us from God, or do we recognize them but attribute the source to something more tangible and easier to contemplate? There is no such thing as 'fate'; it is all God's plan.

Reflection

What seems impossible to human beings is possible to God. God protected the child, Jesus, when he was exposed to mortal danger. Would he not protect us also if he wants to, from any imminent danger to us, if we completely trust him?

Chapter 3
John the Baptist

This chapter considers the life and death of John the Baptist, the forerunner of Jesus. John the Baptist is introduced here purely because of his strong connection to Jesus.

Learning Outcome

- know where and how John the Baptist grew up
- know what John's mission was
- know why and how John was killed

The Life and Preaching of John the Baptist

The Preaching of John the Baptist

And the child grew, and waxed strong in spirit, and was in the deserts till the day of his shewing unto Israel.
(Luke 1: 80 KJV)

Now in the fifteenth year of the reign of Tiberius Caesar, Pontius Pilate being governor of Judaea, and Herod being tetrarch of Galilee, and his brother Philip tetrarch of Ituraea and of the region of Trachonitis, and Lysanias the tetrarch of Abilene,

Annas and Caiaphas being the high priests, the word of God came unto John the son of Zacharias in the wilderness.

And he came into all the country about Jordan, preaching the baptism of repentance for the remission of sins;
(Luke 3: 1-3 KJV)

For this is he that was spoken of by the prophet Esaias, saying, the voice of one crying in the wilderness, prepare ye the way of the Lord, make his paths straight.

And the same John had his raiment of camel's hair, and a leathern girdle about his loins; and his meat was locusts and wild honey.

Then went out to him, Jerusalem and all Judaea, and all the region round about Jordan,

And were baptized of him in Jordan, confessing their sins.
(Matthew 3: 3-6 KJV)

But when he saw many of the Pharisees and Sadducees come to his baptism, he said unto them, O generation of vipers, who hath warned you to flee from the wrath to come?

Bring forth therefore fruits meet for repentance:

And think not to say within yourselves, We have Abraham to our father: for I say unto you, that God is able of these stones to raise up children unto Abraham.

And now also the axe is laid unto the root of the trees: therefore, every tree which bringeth not forth good fruit is hewn down and cast into the fire.
(Matthew 3: 7- 10 KJV)

And the people asked him, saying, what shall we do then?

He answereth and saith unto them, He that hath two coats, let him impart to him that hath none; and he that hath meat, let him do likewise.

Then came also publicans to be baptized, and said unto him, Master, what shall we do?

And he said unto them, Exact no more than that which is appointed you.

And the soldiers likewise demanded of him, saying, and what shall we do? And he said unto them, do violence to no man, neither accuse any falsely; and be content with your wages.

And as the people were in expectation, and all men mused in their hearts of John, whether he were the Christ, or not;

John answered, saying unto them all, I indeed baptize you with water; but one mightier than I cometh, the latchet of whose shoes I am not worthy to unloose: he shall baptize you with the Holy Ghost and with fire:

Whose fan is in his hand, and he will thoroughly purge his floor, and will gather the wheat into his garner; but the chaff he will burn with fire unquenchable.

And many other things in his exhortation preached he unto the people. (Luke 3: 10-18 KJV)

The Death of John the Baptist

But when Herod's birthday was kept, the daughter of Herodias danced before them, and pleased Herod.

Whereupon he promised with an oath to give her whatsoever she would ask.

And she, being before instructed of her mother, said, Give me here John Baptist's head in a charger.

And the king was sorry: nevertheless, for the oath's sake, and them which sat with him at meat, he commanded it to be given her.

And he sent, and beheaded John in the prison.
(Matthew 14: 6-10 KJV)

Focus Questions

1.	Where did John spend his growing up years?	5.	What is special about Jesus' baptism by John?[
2	What was John's food?	6	Why did John reprimand Governor Herod?
3.	What clothes did John wear?	7.	How did John the Baptist die?
4.	What was John popular for among the people?	8	What was the mission of John the Baptist?

Note:

John the Baptist preached similar principles to those of Jesus and was instrumental in preparing Mankind for the revelations that Jesus was to provide. Jesus' baptism by John demonstrates his humility. John's baptism of the people was by water only. When Jesus was baptized by John, we see the power of the Holy Spirit descending upon him. That's why today we believe that during baptism everyone is anointed by the Holy Spirit, their sins are forgiven, and they become children of God.

Reflection

John the Baptist introduced Jesus to the world, making perhaps one of the most significant introductions of all time. Should we not also carry on this tradition by introducing Jesus to our world by our words and deeds?

Chapter 4
The Early Years of Jesus

This chapter deals with the little we know of the Youth days of Jesus.

Learning Outcome

- know where Jesus grew up
- know what Jesus did up to the age of 12 years

Life of Jesus in Nazareth

And when they had performed all things according to the law of the Lord, they returned into Galilee, to their own city Nazareth.
(Luke 2: 39 KJV)

He spent his youth days in Synagogues with elders reading scriptures and lived a life of obedience to his father and mother.

Jesus learned the carpentry trade from his father Joseph and lived in the area of Nazareth most of His early years.

Jesus in the Temple with Jewish Teachers

Now his parents went to Jerusalem every year at the feast of the Passover.

And when he was twelve years old, they went up to Jerusalem after the custom of the feast.

And when they had fulfilled the days, as they returned, the child Jesus tarried behind in Jerusalem; and Joseph and his mother knew not of it.

But they, supposing him to have been in the company, went a day's journey; and they sought him among their kinsfolk and acquaintance.

And when they found him not, they turned back again to Jerusalem, seeking him.

And it came to pass, that after three days they found him in the temple, sitting in the midst of the doctors, both hearing them, and asking them questions.

And all that heard him were astonished at his understanding and answers.

And when they saw him, they were amazed: and his mother said unto him, Son, why hast thou thus dealt with us? behold, thy father and I have sought thee sorrowing.

And he said unto them, how is it that ye sought me? wist ye not that I must be about my Father's business?

And they understood not the saying which he spoke unto them.

And he went down with them, and came to Nazareth, and was subject unto them: but his mother kept all these sayings in her heart.
(Luke 2: 41-51 KJV)

Focus Questions

1	Where did Jesus spend much of his youth?	4	What was Jesus doing in the synagogue?
2	What characteristic of child Jesus can young children follow?	5	After how many days did Joseph and Mary find the lost Jesus?]
3	To what festival Jesus went with his parents every year when he was young?	6	What work did Joseph do for living?

Note:

Jesus' obedience characterized his early infancy. He was obedient to his parents, to the Law and to the government. His obedience was an authentication of his person.

The absence of other details about the early years in the life of Jesus is understandable because he became noticeable only when he started his public ministry.

Reflection

Jesus was God in the flesh and yet He demonstrated respect and obedience to his physical parents when He was with them. He presents a role model for young children in today's society.

The Teachings
of
Jesus

Chapter 5
Jesus Begins Public Life

After 18 years of seclusion, Jesus made the first appearance of His public life at the Jordan River, where John was baptizing.

Learning Outcome

- know who baptized Jesus and where
- know where Jesus first began preaching
- know the names of Jesus' first four disciples
- know the details of the devil's temptation of Jesus
- know the details of Jesus' first miracle
- know why Jesus chased the traders in the Temple
- know the message Jesus gave Nicodemus
- know the message Jesus gave the Samaritan woman

The Baptism of Jesus by John

Then cometh Jesus from Galilee to Jordan unto John, to be baptized of him.

But John forbad him, saying, I have need to be baptized of thee, and comest thou to me?

And Jesus answering said unto him, suffer it to be so now: for thus it becometh us to fulfil all righteousness. Then he suffered him.

And Jesus, when he was baptized, went up straightway out of the water: and, lo, the heavens were opened unto him, and he saw the Spirit of God descending like a dove, and lighting upon him:

And lo a voice from heaven, saying, This is my beloved Son, in whom I am well pleased.
(Matthew 3: 13-17 KJV)

John was known as 'the Baptist' from his practice of preaching and baptizing in the River Jordan. 'Baptism' is a ceremony by which one is initiated and purified. John is the one who recognized Jesus as the messiah. John knew about Jesus' preaching and teaching, believing that his own purpose was to prepare people to listen to Jesus. When Jesus asked John to baptize him, John was taken aback, because he believed that Jesus was the Son of god. The baptism of Jesus marked the beginning of his life as a teacher.

John's Question Answered by Jesus

Now when John had heard in the prison the works of Christ, he sent two of his disciples,

And said unto him, Art thou he that should come, or do we look for another?

Jesus answered and said unto them, Go and shew John again those things which ye do hear and see:

The blind receive their sight, and the lame walk, the lepers are cleansed, and the deaf hear, the dead are raised up, and the poor have the gospel preached to them.

And blessed is he, whosoever shall not be offended in me.!
(Matthew 11: 2-6 KJV)

Jesus Praises John the Baptist

And as they departed, Jesus began to say unto the multitudes concerning John, what went ye out into the wilderness to see? A reed shaken with the wind?

But what went ye out for to see? A man clothed in soft raiment? behold, they that wear soft clothing are in kings' houses.

But what went ye out for to see? A prophet? yea, I say unto you, and more than a prophet.

For this is he, of whom it is written, Behold, I send my messenger before thy face, which shall prepare thy way before thee.

Verily I say unto you, among them that are born of women there hath not risen a greater than John the Baptist: notwithstanding he that is least in the kingdom of heaven is greater than he.

And from the days of John the Baptist until now the kingdom of heaven suffereth violence, and the violent take it by force.

For all the prophets and the law prophesied until John.

And if ye will receive it, this is Elias, which was for to come.

He that hath ears to hear, let him hear.

But whereunto shall I liken this generation? It is like unto children sitting in the markets, and calling unto their fellows,

And saying, we have piped unto you, and ye have not danced; we have mourned unto you, and ye have not lamented.

For John came neither eating nor drinking, and they say, He hath a devil.

The Son of man came eating and drinking, and they say, Behold a man gluttonous, and a winebibber, a friend of publicans and sinners. But wisdom is justified of her children.
(Matthew 11: 7-19 KJV)

Temptation of Jesus

And Jesus being full of the Holy Ghost returned from Jordan, and was led by the Spirit into the wilderness,

Being forty days tempted of the devil. And in those days, he did eat nothing: and when they were ended, he afterward hungered.

And the devil said unto him, if thou be the Son of God, command this stone that it be made bread.

And Jesus answered him, saying, It is written, That man shall not live by bread alone, but by every word of God.

And the devil, taking him up into a high mountain, shewed unto him all the kingdoms of the world in a moment of time.

And the devil said unto him, all this power will I give thee, and the glory of them: for that is delivered unto me; and to whomsoever I will I give it.

If thou therefore wilt worship me, all shall be thine.

And Jesus answered and said unto him, get thee behind me, Satan: for it is written, Thou shalt worship the Lord thy God, and him only shalt thou serve.

And he brought him to Jerusalem, and set him on a pinnacle of the temple, and said unto him, If thou be the Son of God, cast thyself down from hence:

For it is written, He shall give his angels charge over thee, to keep thee:

And in their hands, they shall bear thee up, lest at any time thou dash thy foot against a stone.

And Jesus answering said unto him, It is said, Thou shalt not tempt the Lord thy God.

And when the devil had ended all the temptation, he departed from him for a season.
(Luke 4: 1-13 KJV)

Jesus Begins Preaching in Galilee

From that time Jesus began to preach, and to say, Repent: for the kingdom of heaven is at hand.
(Matthew 4: 17 KJV)

Jesus Calls His First Four Disciples

Now as he walked by the sea of Galilee, he saw Simon and Andrew his brother casting a net into the sea: for they were fishers.

And Jesus said unto them, come ye after me, and I will make you to become fishers of men.

And straightway they forsook their nets and followed him.

And when he had gone a little farther thence, he saw James the son of Zebedee, and John his brother, who also were in the ship mending their nets.

And straightway he called them: and they left their father Zebedee in the ship with the hired servants and went after him.
(Mark 1: 16-20 KJV)

A Wedding at Cana in Galilee (Miracle 1)

On the third day a wedding took place at Cana in Galilee. Jesus' mother was there, and Jesus and his disciples had also been invited to the wedding

When the wine was gone, Jesus' mother said to him, "They have no more wine."

"Woman, why do you involve me?" Jesus replied. "My hour has not yet come."

His mother said to the servants, "Do whatever he tells you." Nearby stood six stone water jars, the kind used by the Jews for ceremonial washing, each holding from twenty to thirty gallons.

Jesus said to the servants, "Fill the jars with water"; so, they filled them to the brim.

Then he told them, "Now draw some out and take it to the master of the banquet."

They did so, and the master of the banquet tasted the water that had been turned into wine. He did not realize where it had come from, though the servants who had drawn the water knew.

Then he called the bridegroom aside and said, "Everyone brings out the choice wine first and then the cheaper wine after the guests have had too much to drink; but you have saved the best till now."

What Jesus did here in Cana of Galilee was the first of the signs through which he revealed his glory; and his disciples believed in him.
(John 2: 1-11 KJV)

Jesus Chases Traders from the Temple

And the Jews' Passover was at hand, and Jesus went up to Jerusalem.

And found in the temple those that sold oxen and sheep and doves, and the changers of money sitting:

And when he had made a scourge of small cords, he drove them all out of the temple, and the sheep, and the oxen; and poured out the changers' money, and overthrew the tables;

And said unto them that sold doves, take these things hence; make not my Father's house an house of merchandise.

And his disciples remembered that it was written, the zeal of thine house hath eaten me up.

Then answered the Jews and said unto him, what sign shewest thou unto us, seeing that thou doest these things?

Jesus answered and said unto them, destroy this temple, and in three days I will raise it up.

Then said the Jews, Forty and six years was this temple in building, and wilt thou rear it up in three days?

But he spoke of the temple of his body.
(John 2: 13-21 KJV)

Jesus Meets a Jewish Leader - Nicodemus

There was a man of the Pharisees, named Nicodemus, a ruler of the Jews:

The same came to Jesus by night, and said unto him, Rabbi, we know that thou art a teacher come from God: for no man can do these miracles that thou doest, except God be with him.

Jesus answered and said unto him, Verily, verily, I say unto thee, except a man be born again, he cannot see the kingdom of God.

Nicodemus saith unto him, How can a man be born when he is old? can he enter the second time into his mother's womb, and be born?

Jesus answered, Verily, verily, I say unto thee, except a man be born of water and of the Spirit, he cannot enter into the kingdom of God.

That which is born of the flesh is flesh; and that which is born of the Spirit is spirit.

Marvel not that I said unto thee, Ye must be born again.

The wind bloweth where it listeth, and thou hearest the sound thereof, but canst not tell whence it cometh, and whither it goeth: so is every one that is born of the Spirit.

Nicodemus answered and said unto him, how can these things be?

Jesus answered and said unto him, Art thou a master of Israel, and knowest not these things?

Verily, verily, I say unto thee, We speak that we do know, and testify that we have seen; and ye receive not our witness.

If I have told you earthly things, and ye believe not, how shall ye believe, if I tell you of heavenly things?

And no man hath ascended up to heaven, but he that came down from heaven, even the Son of man which is in heaven.

And as Moses lifted up the serpent in the wilderness, even so must the Son of man be lifted up:

That whosoever believeth in him should not perish but have eternal life.

For God so loved the world, that he gave his only begotten Son, that whosoever believeth in him should not perish, but have everlasting life.

For God sent not his Son into the world to condemn the world; but that the world through him might be saved.

He that believeth on him is not condemned: but he that believeth not is condemned already, because he hath not believed in the name of the only begotten Son of God.

And this is the condemnation, that light is come into the world, and men loved darkness rather than light, because their deeds were evil.

For everyone that doeth evil hateth the light, neither cometh to the light, lest his deeds should be reproved.

But he that doeth truth cometh to the light, that his deeds may be made manifest, that they are wrought in God.
(John 3: 1-21 KJV)

Jesus and the Samaritan Woman

When therefore the Lord knew how the Pharisees had heard that Jesus made and baptized more disciples than John,
(Though Jesus himself baptized not, but his disciples,)

He left Judaea and departed again into Galilee.

And he must needs go through Samaria.

Then cometh he to a city of Samaria, which is called Sychar, near to the parcel of ground that Jacob gave to his son Joseph.

Now Jacob's well was there. Jesus, therefore, being wearied with his journey, sat thus on the well: and it was about the sixth hour.

There cometh a woman of Samaria to draw water: Jesus saith unto her, give me to drink.

(For his disciples were gone away unto the city to buy meat.)

Then saith the woman of Samaria unto him, how is it that thou, being a Jew, askest drink of me, which am a woman of Samaria? for the Jews have no dealings with the Samaritans.

Jesus answered and said unto her, If thou knewest the gift of God, and who it is that saith to thee, Give me to drink; thou wouldest have asked of him, and he would have given thee living water. The woman saith unto him, Sir, thou hast nothing to draw with, and the well is deep: from whence then hast thou that living water?

Art thou greater than our father Jacob, which gave us the well, and drank thereof himself, and his children, and his cattle?

Jesus answered and said unto her, whosoever drinketh of this water shall thirst again:

But whosoever drinketh of the water that I shall give him shall never thirst; but the water that I shall give him shall be in him a well of water springing up into everlasting life.

The woman saith unto him, Sir, give me this water, that I thirst not, neither come hither to draw.

Jesus saith unto her, Go, call thy husband, and come hither.

The woman answered and said, I have no husband. Jesus said unto her, Thou hast well said, I have no husband:

For thou hast had five husbands; and he whom thou now hast is not thy husband: in that saidst thou truly.

The woman saith unto him, Sir, I perceive that thou art a prophet.

Our fathers worshipped in this mountain; and ye say, that in Jerusalem is the place where men ought to worship.

Jesus saith unto her, Woman, believe me, the hour cometh, when ye shall neither in this mountain, nor yet at Jerusalem, worship the Father.

Ye worship ye know not what: we know what we worship: for salvation is of the Jews.

But the hour cometh, and now is, when the true worshippers shall worship the Father in spirit and in truth: for the Father seeketh such to worship him.

God is a Spirit: and they that worship him must worship him in spirit and in truth.

The woman saith unto him, I know that Messiah cometh, which is called Christ: when he is come, he will tell us all things.

Jesus saith unto her, I that speak unto thee am he.

And upon this came his disciples, and marveled that he talked with the woman: yet no man said, What seekest thou? or, Why talkest thou with her?

The woman then left her waterpot, and went her way into the city, and saith to the men,

Come, see a man, which told me all things that ever I did: is not this the Christ?

Then they went out of the city and came unto him.

In the mean while his disciples prayed him, saying, Master, eat.

But he said unto them, I have meat to eat that ye know not of. Therefore, said the disciples one to another, Hath any man brought him ought to eat?

Jesus saith unto them, my meat is to do the will of him that sent me, and to finish his work.

Say not ye, there are yet four months, and then cometh harvest? behold, I say unto you, Lift up your eyes, and look on the fields; for they are white already to harvest.

And he that reapeth receiveth wages, and gathereth fruit unto life eternal: that both he that soweth and he that reapeth may rejoice together.

And herein is that saying true, One soweth, and another reapeth.

I sent you to reap that whereon ye bestowed no labor: other men labored, and ye are entered into their labors.

And many of the Samaritans of that city believed on him for the saying of the woman, which testified, He told me all that ever I did.

So, when the Samaritans were come unto him, they besought him that he would tarry with them: and he abode there two days.

And many more believed because of his own word;

And said unto the woman, now we believe, not because of thy saying: for we have heard him ourselves, and know that this is indeed the Christ, the Savior of the world.
(John 4: 1-42 KJV)

Focus Questions

1	Where did John baptize Jesus?	6	Who are the first four disciples of Jesus?
2	What question did John ask Jesus?	7	What was Jesus' first miracle and where did it happen?
3	How did Jesus praise John the Baptist?	8	Why did Jesus chase traders from the temple?
4	How did the devil tempt Jesus and what answers did Jesus give?	9	What did Jesus mean when he told Nicodemus that 'man must be born again'?
5	Where did Jesus begin preaching?	10	What did Jesus mean when he told the Samaritan woman at the well 'those who drink the water I give will never be thirsty again'?

Note:

Other than what Jesus did at the age of twelve, nothing else is known about his life until he was 30 years old. Jesus was the most important person to have set foot on Earth and yet no one was appointed by God to keep track of his formative years. Jesus was missing for eighteen years but suddenly emerged at the age of 30 to perform miracles and to teach about the Kingdom of Heaven and guide us to seek for an everlasting life in his kingdom.

He said, "I am the light of the world and he who follows me will not walk in darkness but will have the light of life."

Reflection

Jesus began changing the way Man's relationship to God was viewed, and he signaled a period of new thinking, of re-aligning how faith and religion should be practiced. Are they practiced today, the way he intended?

Chapter 6
Miracles Continue in Galilee

Now after two days he departed thence and went into Galilee.

For Jesus himself testified, that a prophet hath no honor in his own country.

Then when he was coming into Galilee, the Galileans received him, having seen all the things that he did at Jerusalem at the feast: for they also went unto the feast.
(John 4: 43-45 KJV)

Learning Outcome

- know the details of some of the miracles Jesus performed
- know the key words Jesus used when performing miracle
- know how Jesus enlisted Matthew.

Jesus Heals an Official's Son (Miracle 2)

So Jesus came again into Cana of Galilee, where he made the water wine. And there was a certain nobleman, whose son was sick at Capernaum.

When he heard that Jesus was come out of Judaea into Galilee, he went unto him, and besought him that he would come down, and heal his son: for he was at the point of death.

Then said Jesus unto him, except ye see signs and wonders, ye will not believe.

The nobleman saith unto him, Sir, come down here my child die.

Jesus saith unto him, Go thy way; thy son liveth. And the man believed the word that Jesus had spoken unto him, and he went his way.

And as he was now going down, his servants met him, and told him, saying, Thy son liveth.

Then enquired he of them the hour when he began to amend. And they said unto him, yesterday at the seventh hour the fever left him.

So, the father knew that it was at the same hour, in the which Jesus said unto him, thy son liveth: and himself believed, and his whole house. (John 4: 46-53 KJV)

Jesus Orders an Evil Spirit Out (Miracle 3)

And came down to Capernaum, a city of Galilee, and taught them on the sabbath days.

And they were astonished at his doctrine: for his word was with power.

And in the synagogue, there was a man, which had a spirit of an unclean devil, and cried out with a loud voice, Saying, let us alone;

what have we to do with thee, thou Jesus of Nazareth? art thou come to destroy us? I know thee who thou art; the Holy One of God.

And Jesus rebuked him, saying, hold thy peace, and come out of him.

And when the devil had thrown him in the midst, he came out of him, and hurt him not.
(Luke 4: 31-35 KJV)

Jesus heals Simon's Mother-in-law (Miracle 4)

And he arose out of the synagogue and entered into Simon's house. And Simon's wife's mother was taken with a great fever; and they besought him for her.

And he stood over her and rebuked the fever; and it left her: and immediately she arose and ministered unto them.
(Luke 4: 38-39 KJV)

Jesus Heals a Man with Skin Disease (Miracle 5)

When he was coming down from the mountain, great multitudes followed him.

And, behold, there came a leper and worshipped him, saying, Lord, if thou wilt, thou canst make me clean.

And Jesus put forth his hand, and touched him, saying, I will; be thou clean. And immediately his leprosy was cleansed.

And Jesus saith unto him, See thou tell no man; but go thy way, shew thyself to the priest, and offer the gift that Moses commanded, for a testimony unto them.
(Matthew 8: 1-4 KJV)

Jesus Heals a Paralytic (Miracle 6)

And it came to pass on a certain day, as he was teaching, that there were Pharisees and doctors of the law sitting by, which were come out of every town of Galilee, and Judaea, and Jerusalem: and the power of the Lord was present to heal them.

And, behold, men brought in a bed a man which was taken with a palsy: and they sought means to bring him in, and to lay him before him.

And when they could not find by what way they might bring him in because of the multitude, they went upon the housetop, and let him down through the tiling with his couch into the midst before Jesus.

And when he saw their faith, he said unto him, Man, thy sins are forgiven thee.

And the scribes and the Pharisees began to reason, saying, who is this which speaketh blasphemies? Who can forgive sins, but God alone?

But when Jesus perceived their thoughts, he answering said unto them, What reason ye in your hearts?

Whether is easier, to say, thy sins be forgiven thee; or to say, Rise up and walk?

But that ye may know that the Son of man hath power upon earth to forgive sins, (he said unto the sick of the palsy,) I say unto thee, Arise, and take up thy couch, and go into thine house.

And immediately he rose up before them, and took up that whereon he lay, and departed to his own house, glorifying God
(Luke 5: 17-25 KJV)

And as Jesus passed forth from thence, he saw a man, named Matthew, sitting at the receipt of custom: and he saith unto him, Follow me. And he arose and followed him.

And it came to pass, as Jesus sat at meat in the house, behold, many publicans and sinners came and sat down with him and his disciples.

And when the Pharisees saw it, they said unto his disciples, Why eateth your Master with publicans and sinners?

But when Jesus heard that, he said unto them, they that be whole need not a physician, but they that are sick.

But go ye and learn what that meaneth, I will have mercy, and not sacrifice for I am not come to call the righteous, but sinners to repentance. (Matthew 9: 9-13 KJV)

Focus Questions

1	What did the government official want Jesus to do for him?	4	What words did Jesus utter when he cured the paralytic?
2	What words did Jesus use when he ordered the evil spirit to come out of the man?	5	What did Jesus tell the man with the skin disease after healing him?]
3	What did Jesus cure Simon's mother-in-law of?	6	What was Matthew doing when Jesus asked to follow him?

Note:

The miracles of Jesus were not random acts, but they carried a specific message to the nation of Israel, the Jews, and to all people. Jesus used his power to perform miraculous acts of humanity and compassion, showing that God was a compassionate being, and that His Will could overcome earthly constraints. The miracles provide a window into faith – if the impossible can happen, does this not mean the world as we see it is only a fraction of what can be seen if we truly open our eyes?

Reflection

The people who were cured of their diseases had complete faith that Jesus could heal them. They were persistent in asking Jesus to heal them. God listens because he is compassionate and is a powerful being. Rather than sink in misery under the things that ail us, we should adopt a more optimistic view of life, and have faith that miracles can happen if we believe in them. But miracles need our persistence too, and we are an integral part of these miracles. If we do not endeavor, believe and retain a positive outlook, we cannot receive these miracles.

Chapter 7
Questions Answered by Jesus

Jesus answers questions about working and healing on the Sabbath day and performs more miracles.

Learning Outcome

- know what Sabbath is.
- know what Jesus taught about Sabbath

The Meaning of Sabbath

The Sabbath was the consecration of the seventh day of the week, namely, Saturday, to God as the Creator of the universe. It is customary to keep this day holy or at least minimize working for one's own ends and interests and devote time to God by special acts of positive worship.

According to the Old Testament, God wanted us to worship him on Saturdays. However, worship these days is done by some on Saturdays and others on Sundays! Sunday is being called the Lord's day.

The Question About Fasting - Mixing the Old and the New (Parable 1)

And they said unto him, why do the disciples of John fast often, and make prayers, and likewise the disciples of the Pharisees; but thine eat and drink?

And he said unto them, can ye make the children of the bridechamber fast, while the bridegroom is with them?

But the days will come, when the bridegroom shall be taken away from them, and then shall they fast in those days.

And he spoke also a parable unto them; No man putteth a piece of a new garment upon an old; if otherwise, then both the new maketh a rent, and the piece that was taken out of the new agreeth not with the old.

And no man putteth new wine into old bottles; else the new wine will burst the bottles, and be spilled, and the bottles shall perish.

But new wine must be put into new bottles; and both are preserved. No man also having drunk old wine straightway desireth new: for he saith, the old is better.
(Luke 5: 33-39 KJV)

What Jesus was trying to portray is purity. He wants us not to be mixed with anything else. God wants our focus solely on Him, not to be distracted by worldly pleasures or the satisfaction of others.

While he spoke these things unto them, behold, there came a **certain ruler,** and worshipped him, saying, my daughter is even now dead: but come and lay thy hand upon her, and she shall live.

And Jesus arose, and followed him, and so did his disciples.

And, behold, **a woman, which was diseased with an issue of blood** twelve years, came behind him, and touched the hem of his garment:

For she said within herself, If I may but touch his garment, I shall be whole.

But Jesus turned him about, and when he saw her, he said, Daughter, be of good comfort; thy faith hath made thee whole. And the woman was made whole from that hour.
(Miracle 7)

And when Jesus came into the ruler's house, and saw the minstrels and the people making a noise,

He said unto them, give place: for the maid is not dead, but sleepeth. And they laughed him to scorn.

But when the people were put forth, he went in, and took her by the hand, and the maid arose.

And the fame hereof went abroad into all that land.
(Miracle 8)
(Matthew 9: 18-26 KJV)

And when Jesus departed thence, **two blind men** followed him, crying, and saying, thou son of David, have mercy on us.

And when he was come into the house, the blind men came to him: and Jesus saith unto them, believe ye that I am able to do this? They said unto him, Yea, Lord.

Then touched he their eyes, saying, according to your faith be it unto you.

And their eyes were opened; and Jesus straitly charged them, saying, see that no man know it.

But they, when they were departed, spread abroad his fame in all that country.
(Miracle 9)
(Matthew 9: 27-31 KJV)

As they went out, behold, they brought to him a **dumb man possessed with a devil.**

And when the devil was cast out, the dumb spoke: and the multitudes marveled, saying, It was never so seen in Israel.

But the Pharisees said, "He casteth out devils through the prince of the devils."
(Miracle10)
(Matthew 9: 32-34 KJV)

There are thirty-five separate miracles that were performed by Jesus as recorded in the Gospels. However, these are not all of the miracles that Jesus performed. There are twelve occasions mentioned in Matthew (15:30), when Jesus performed several wonderful works where great crowds went to him taking the lame, the blind, the crippled, the mute and many others, and laid them at his feet "and he healed them"

The Question About Picking Wheat on Sabbath

And it came to pass, that he went through the corn fields on the sabbath day; and his disciples began, as they went*, to pluck the ears of corn.

And the Pharisees said unto him, Behold, why do they on the sabbath day that which is not lawful?

And he said unto them, Have ye never read what David did, when he had need, and was an hungred, he, and they that were with him?

How he went into the house of God in the days of Abiathar the high priest, and did eat the shewbread*, which is not lawful to eat but for the priests, and gave also to them which were with him?

And he said unto them, The sabbath was made for man, and not man for the sabbath:

Therefore the Son of man is Lord also of the sabbath.
(Mark 2: 23-28 KJV)

The Question About Healing on Sabbath

And when he was departed thence, he went into their synagogue:

And, behold, there was a man which had his hand withered. And they asked him, saying, is it lawful to heal on the sabbath days? that they might accuse him.

And he said unto them, What man shall there be among you, that shall have one sheep, and if it falls into a pit on the sabbath day, will he not lay hold on it, and lift it out?

How much then is a man better than a sheep? Wherefore it is lawful to do well on the sabbath days.

Then saith he to the man, Stretch forth thine hand. And he stretched it forth; and it was restored whole, like as the other.

Then the Pharisees went out, and held a council against him, how they might destroy him.
(Matthew 12: 9 -14 KJV)

But when Jesus knew it, he withdrew himself from thence: and great multitudes followed him, and he healed them all;

And charged them that they should not make him known:

That it might be fulfilled which was spoken by Esaias the prophet, saying,

Behold my servant, whom I have chosen; my beloved, in whom my soul is well pleased: I will put my spirit upon him, and he shall shew judgment to the Gentiles.

He shall not strive, nor cry; neither shall any man hear his voice in the streets.

A bruised reed shall he not break, and smoking flax shall he not quench, till he send forth judgment unto victory.

And in his name shall the Gentiles trust.
(Matthew 12: 15-21 KJV)

Focus Questions

1	What do you understand by 'Sabbath"?	5	How did Jesus explain the meaning of: "The Sabbath was made for the good of human beings; they were not made for the Sabbath":
2	What reply did Jesus give when he was questioned why his disciples eat and drink always instead of fasting frequently?	6	What answer did Jesus give when he was asked: "Is it against our law to heal on the Sabbath?"
3	What is the significance of the parable of 'mixing the old and the new'?	7	What could be the reason for Jesus telling the persons he healed 'Don't tell this to anyone'?
4.	To whom did Jesus say "Courage, my daughter! Your faith has made you well."	8.	Give one reason why the Jews wanted to kill Jesus?

Note:

Pharisees refused to recognize Jesus as God's Messenger, sent to re-launch the Kingdom of God. They gave more importance to rules and religious practices than showing compassion and caring for human needs. Jesus provided some interesting answers to the Pharisees' questions about his decision to follow what they considered as Law. Perhaps he is suggesting that we should follow laws that are in the best interest of humans rather than blindly following any conventions and false pious practices.

'Love one another as I have loved you' are some of the best words spoken by Jesus to guide us during our life on earth. Not a law or a rule! It is an attitude and a behavior to reflect our faith in Jesus.

Reflection

When God asked us to remember the Sabbath day He did so because He wanted to help the relationship between him and us grow. Hence the traditional Sabbath observance is based on the authority of God's Word. However, practices have changed with the changing times. If God made a perpetual weekly schedule for us to commune with Him, should we not follow that strictly?

Chapter 8
The Twelve Apostles of Jesus

This chapter gives a brief account of the 12 apostles of Jesus. The apostles went around with Jesus during the entire period of his ministry. They continued to spread the 'Good News' till their lives ended.

Learning Outcome

- know how Jesus recruited his 12 apostles
- know where the apostles spread the 'Good News'
- know the circumstances under which the lives of apostles ended.

Jesus Chooses 12 Apostles from His Disciples

Disciples were people who followed JESUS and listened to his teachings. They called him *rabbi*, which means "Teacher". The two words 'disciples' and 'apostles' are used interchangeably. In a true sense, the 12 disciples who received a mission directly from Jesus are called apostles. So, Jesus' 12 apostles are disciples but not all his disciples are apostles.

And he goeth up into a mountain, and calleth unto him whom he would: and they came unto him.

And he ordained twelve, that they should be with him, and that he might send them forth to preach,

And to have power to heal sicknesses, and to cast out devils:

And Simon he surnamed Peter;

And James the son of Zebedee, and John the brother of James; and he surnamed them Boanerges, which is, The sons of thunder:

And Andrew, and Philip, and Bartholomew, and Matthew, and Thomas, and James the son of Alphaeus, and Thaddaeus, and Simon the Canaanite,

And Judas Iscariot, which also betrayed him: and they went into an house. (Mark 3: 13-19 KJV)

Apostle Profile

PETER

The apostle who denied JESUS three times but later became a "Rock"; Also known as Simon or Cephas, spent his last days in Rome where he was beheaded. He wrote the Epistles (Peter 1 & 2). He ministered mostly among the Jews to proclaim the good news.

ANDREW

Brother of Peter and one of the first apostles of Jesus. He did his ministry in present day Russia and was martyred at Patros.

JAMES

Son of Zebadee and brother of John. Not much is known about his ministry. He was martyred by king Herod Agrippa (Acts 12).

JOHN

Son of Zebadee and brother of James. The beloved disciple of Jesus, who ministered with Peter. He is the only apostle who was not martyred. He wrote the gospel of John, the three epistles (John 1,2 & 3). He also wrote the book of Revelation while in exile in the island of Patmos.

PHILIP

Philip ministered in Samaria and also preached the good news to the Ethiopian official, who carried the message about Jesus to Ethiopia.

NATHANIEL (Bartholomew)

Introduced to Jesus by Philip (John 1:45). No details are available regarding his ministry. Some say that he went to India, some say he went to Armenia while others say he ministered with Phillip as they were friends.

MATTHEW

A former tax-collector who became a disciple of Jesus. His gospel is mainly for the Jews to prove that Jesus was the promised Messiah.

THOMAS

Famously known as the "doubting Thomas", he established churches in Babylon and Persis. There is a tradition that Thomas went to India to preach the Good News, where he was martyred. He is also said to have established a church in China.

JAMES (Son of Alpheus)

Brother of apostle Matthew. Not much is known about his ministry although some claim that he was ministering in Syria. He was martyred by stoning while preaching about Jesus.

SIMON (The Zealot) – the anti-Roman fanatic

He attempted to overthrow the Romans by using violence. Simon joined Jesus in the hope that Jesus came to deliver Israel from Roman power. Later preached in North Africa. Some say that he was martyred in Persia.

JUDE (Thaddeus)

Not to be confused with Jude the half-brother of Jesus (who also wrote the letter of Jude). He ministered in Armenia, Northern Persia and Syria. He was martyred in Modern day Iran.

JUDAS ISCARIOT

He was in-charge of finances of the Apostles and the one who betrayed Jesus for 30 pieces of silver and later hung himself. (Later he was replaced by Matthias).

Focus Questions

1	What is the difference between a disciple and an apostle?	7	Who is considered as the favorite apostle of Jesus?
2	Who are the first chosen apostles of Jesus?	8	Where did Apostle Thomas establish churches first?
3	What are the names of the third and fourth apostles Jesus recruited?	9	What do you know of the other Simon?
4	What name did Jesus give to the apostle Simon?	10	How and why did Judas Iscariot commit suicide?
5	What is the name of Simon's brother who is also an apostle?	11	Which of the Apostles wrote the Gospels?
6	Who are the other apostles who are brothers as well?	12	What is the name of the Apostle who replaced Judas Iscariot?

Note:

The apostles were fortunate to have witnessed for themselves the extraordinary events during the ministry of Jesus. Despite this, their human traits still led some of them to deny, doubt and betray Jesus. The challenge for us today is to believe in Jesus without the convincing proof described in the Bible and accept that our occasional failure in this endeavor is because we are human.

Reflection

The apostles Jesus chose were not rich, famous, educated nor well known in society. He chose the marginalized to spread the Good News. By the power of the Holy Spirit the apostles were transformed into powerful preachers and teachers and were filled with courage and great wisdom.

The Holy Spirit can transform each one of us in ways unimaginable to us, if we accept and obey God's calling in our lives.

Chapter 9
The Sermon on the Mount

Jesus saw the crowds and went up to a hill (a mountain near Capernaum) where he sat down. His disciples gathered around him and he began to teach them:

Learning Outcome

- know Jesus' eight beatitudes
- know what Jesus taught about hatred and anger
- know what Jesus taught about divorce and adultery
- know what Jesus taught about fasting, praying and charity.
- know what Jesus taught about Love and Judging others
- know what Jesus taught about 'trust in God'

The Eight True Happiness (Beatitudes)

- Blessed are the poor in spirit: for theirs is the kingdom of heaven.
- Blessed are they that mourn for they shall be comforted.
- Blessed are the meek: for they shall inherit the earth.
- Blessed are they which do hunger and thirst after righteousness: for they shall be filled.
- Blessed are the merciful: for they shall obtain mercy.
- Blessed are the pure in heart: for they shall see God.
- Blessed are the peacemakers: for they shall be called the children of God.
- Blessed are they which are persecuted for righteousness' sake: for theirs is the kingdom of heaven.

(Matthew 5: 3-10 KJV)

"Poor in spirit" means those who realize that they can never achieve salvation on their own and instead put their complete faith and trust in Jesus.

"Mourn" means crying and regretting for own sins and for the sins of this world

'Humble" means being gentle and kind

"Hunger and thirst for righteousness" means a continuous desire for justice and moral perfection.

"Merciful" is to show Love, compassion, and forgiveness towards one's neighbor.

"Pure of heart" means to be free of all selfish intentions and self-seeking desires.

"Peacemakers" are those who try to bring peace and friendship to others.

"Persecuted for the sake of righteousness" means victimized for following the words of Jesus.

Some Sayings of Jesus

Blessed are ye, when men shall revile you, and persecute you, and shall say all manner of evil against you falsely, for my sake.

Rejoice, and be exceeding glad: for great is your reward in heaven: for so persecuted they the prophets which were before you.

Think not that I am come to destroy the law, or the prophets: I am not come to destroy, but to fulfil.

For verily I say unto you, till heaven and earth pass, one jot or one tittle shall in no wise pass from the law, till all be fulfilled.

Whosoever therefore shall break one of these least commandments, and shall teach men so, he shall be called the least in the kingdom of heaven: but whosoever shall do and teach them, the same shall be called great in the kingdom of heaven.

For I say unto you, that except your righteousness shall exceed the righteousness of the scribes and Pharisees, ye shall in no case enter into the kingdom of heaven.
(Matthew 5: 11-12 and 17-20 KJV)

Points Stressed by Jesus

1. Feel no anger:

Ye have heard that it was said of them of old time, thou shalt not kill; and whosoever shall kill shall be in danger of the judgment:

But I say unto you, that whosoever is angry with his brother without a cause shall be in danger of the judgment: and whosoever shall say to his brother, Raca, shall be in danger of the council: but whosoever shall say, thou fool, shall be in danger of hell fire.
(Matthew 5: 21-22 KJV)

2. Make peace before making offering to God

Therefore, if thou bring thy gift to the altar, and there rememberest that thy brother hath ought against thee;

Leave there thy gift before the altar and go thy way; first be reconciled to thy brother, and then come and offer thy gift.
(Matthew 5: 23-24 KJV)

3. Settle disputes out of courts

Agree with thine adversary quickly, whiles thou art in the way with him; lest at any time the adversary deliver thee to the judge, and the judge deliver thee to the officer, and thou be cast into prison.

Verily I say unto thee, thou shalt by no means come out thence, till thou hast paid the uttermost farthing.
(Matthew 5: 25-26 KJV)

4. Do not commit adultery

Ye have heard that it was said by them of old time, thou shalt not commit adultery:

But I say unto you, that whosoever looketh on a woman to lust after her hath committed adultery with her already in his heart.

And if thy right eye offend thee, pluck it out, and cast it from thee: for it is profitable for thee that one of thy members should perish, and not that thy whole body should be cast into hell.

And if thy right hand offend thee, cut it off, and cast it from thee: for it is profitable for thee that one of thy members should perish, and not that thy whole body should be cast into hell.
(Matthew 5: 27-30 KJV)

5. Divorce may result in adultery

been said, whosoever shall put away his wife, let him give her a writing of divorcement:

But I say unto you, that whosoever shall put away his wife, saving for the cause of fornication, causeth her to commit adultery: and whosoever shall marry her that is divorced committeth adultery.

6. Don't swear

Again, ye have heard that it hath been said by them of old time, thou shalt not forswear thyself, but shalt perform unto the Lord thine oaths:

But I say unto you, swear not at all; neither by heaven; for it is God's throne:

Nor by the earth; for it is his footstool: neither by Jerusalem; for it is the city of the great King.

Neither shalt thou swear by thy head, because thou canst not make one hair white or black.

But let your communication be, Yea, yea; Nay, nay: for whatsoever is more than these cometh of evil.
(Matthew 5: 33-37 KJV)

7. Take no revenge

But I say unto you, that ye resist not evil: but whosoever shall smite thee on thy right cheek, turn to him the other also.

And if any man will sue thee at the law, and take away thy coat, let him have thy cloak also.

And whosoever shall compel thee to go a mile, go with him twain.

Give to him that asketh thee, and from him that would borrow of thee turn not thou away.
(Matthew 5: 39-42 KJV)

8. Love your enemies

Ye have heard that it hath been said, thou shalt love thy neighbor, and hate thine enemy.

But I say unto you, love your enemies, bless them that curse you, do good to them that hate you, and pray for them which despitefully use you, and persecute you;

That ye may be the children of your Father which is in heaven: for he maketh his sun to rise on the evil and on the good, and sendeth rain on the just and on the unjust.

For if ye love them which love you, what reward have ye? do not even the publicans the same?

And if ye salute your brethren only, what do ye more than others? do not even the publicans so?
(Matthew 5: 43-47 KJV)

9. Do no charity publicly

Take heed that ye do not your alms before men, to be seen of them: otherwise ye have no reward of your Father which is in heaven.

Therefore, when thou doest thine alms, do not sound a trumpet before thee, as the hypocrites do in the synagogues and in the streets, that they may have glory of men. Verily I say unto you, they have their reward.

But when thou doest alms, let not thy left hand know what thy right hand doeth:

That thine alms may be in secret: and thy Father which seeth in secret himself shall reward thee openly.
(Matthew 6: 1-4 KJV)

10. Praying method

And when thou prayest, thou shalt not be as the hypocrites are: for they love to pray standing in the synagogues and in the corners of the streets, that they may be seen of men. Verily I say unto you, they have their reward.

But thou, when thou prayest, enter into thy closet, and when thou hast shut thy door, pray to thy Father which is in secret; and thy Father which seeth in secret shall reward thee openly.

But when ye pray, use not vain repetitions, as the heathen do: for they think that they shall be heard for their much speaking.

Be not ye therefore like unto them: for your Father knoweth what things ye have need of, before ye ask him.

After this manner therefore pray ye:

Our Father which art in heaven, hallowed be thy name.

Thy kingdom come, thy will be done in earth, as it is in heaven.

Give us this day our daily bread.

And forgive us our debts, as we forgive our debtors.

And lead us not into temptation but deliver us from evil: For thine is the kingdom, and the power, and the glory, forever. Amen.

For if ye forgive men their trespasses, your heavenly Father will also forgive you:

But if ye forgive not men their trespasses, neither will your Father forgive your trespasses.
(Matthew 6: 5-15 KJV)

11. Fasting method

Moreover, when you fast, do not be like the [a]hypocrites, with a sad countenance. For they disfigure their faces that they may appear to men to be fasting. Assuredly, I say to you, they have their reward. But you, when you fast, anoint your head and wash your face, so that you do not appear to men to be fasting, but to your Father who is in the secret place; and your Father who sees in secret will reward you [b]openly.
(Matthew 6: 16-18 KJV)

12. Store riches in heaven

Lay not up for yourselves treasures upon earth, where moth and rust doth corrupt, and where thieves break through and steal:

But lay up for yourselves treasures in heaven, where neither moth nor rust doth corrupt, and where thieves do not break through nor steal:

For where your treasure is, there will your heart be also.

No man can serve two masters: for either he will hate the one and love the other; or else he will hold to the one and despise the other. Ye cannot serve God and mammon.
(Matthew 6: 19-21 and 24 KJV)

13. Do not worry about food, clothes or tomorrow

Therefore, I say unto you, take no thought for your life, what ye shall eat, or what ye shall drink; nor yet for your body, what ye shall put on. Is not the life more than meat, and the body than raiment?

Behold the fowls of the air: for they sow not, neither do they reap, nor gather into barns; yet your heavenly Father feedeth them. Are ye not much better than they?

Which of you by taking thought can add one cubit unto his stature?

And why take ye thought for raiment? Consider the lilies of the field, how they grow; they toil not, neither do they spin:

And yet I say unto you, that even Solomon in all his glory was not arrayed like one of these.

Wherefore, if God so clothe the grass of the field, which today is, and tomorrow is cast into the oven, shall he not much more clothe you, O ye of little faith?

Therefore, take no thought, saying, what shall we eat? or, What shall we drink? or, Wherewithal shall we be clothed?
(For after all these things do the Gentiles seek:) for your heavenly Father knoweth that ye have need of all these things.

But seek ye first the kingdom of God, and his righteousness; and all these things shall be added unto you.

Take therefore no thought for the morrow: for the morrow shall take thought for the things of itself. Sufficient unto the day is the evil thereof. (Matthew 6: 25-34 KJV)

14. Come to me and rest

Come unto me, all ye that labor and are heavy laden, and I will give you rest.

Take my yoke upon you and learn of me; for I am meek and lowly in heart: and ye shall find rest unto your souls.

For my yoke is easy, and my burden is light.
(Matthew 11: 28-30 KJV)

15. Do not judge others

Judge not, that ye be not judged.

For with what judgment ye judge, ye shall be judged: and with what measure ye mete, it shall be measured to you again.

And why beholdest thou the mote that is in thy brother's eye, but considerest not the beam that is in thine own eye?

Or how wilt thou say to thy brother, let me pull out the mote out of thine eye; and, behold, a beam is in thine own eye?

Thou hypocrite, first cast out the beam out of thine own eye; and then shalt thou see clearly to cast out the mote out of thy brother's eye. (Matthew 7: 1-5 KJV)

16. Ask, Seek, Knock

Ask, and it shall be given you; seek, and ye shall find; knock, and it shall be opened unto you:

For everyone that asketh receiveth; and he that seeketh findeth; and to him that knocketh it shall be opened.

Or what man is there of you, whom if his son ask bread, will he give him a stone?

Or if he ask a fish, will he give him a serpent?

If ye then, being evil, know how to give good gifts unto your children, how much more shall your Father which is in heaven give good things to them that ask him?

Therefore, all things whatsoever ye would that men should do to you, do ye even so to them: for this is the law and the prophets.

(Matthew 7: 7-12 KJV)

17. Go through the narrow gate

Enter ye in at the strait gate: for wide is the gate, and broad is the way, that leadeth to destruction, and many there be which go in there at:

14 Because strait is the gate, and narrow is the way, which leadeth unto life, and few there be that find it.
(Matthew 7: 13-14 KJV)

18. Beware of false prophets

Beware of false prophets, which come to you in sheep's clothing, but inwardly they are ravening wolves.

Ye shall know them by their fruits. Do men gather grapes of thorns, or figs of thistles?

Even so every good tree bringeth forth good fruit; but a corrupt tree bringeth forth evil fruit.

A good tree cannot bring forth evil fruit, neither can a corrupt tree bring forth good fruit.

Every tree that bringeth not forth good fruit is hewn down and cast into the fire.

Wherefore by their fruits ye shall know them.
(Matthew 7: 15-20 KJV)

19. Do what the Father wants

Not everyone that saith unto me, Lord, Lord, shall enter into the kingdom of heaven; but he that doeth the will of my Father which is in heaven. (Matthew 7: 21 KJV)

The Wise and Foolish Builders

Therefore, whosoever heareth these sayings of mine, and doeth them, I will liken him unto a wise man, which built his house upon a rock:

And the rain descended, and the floods came, and the winds blew, and beat upon that house; and it fell not: for it was founded upon a rock.

And everyone that heareth these sayings of mine, and doeth them not, shall be likened unto a foolish man, which built his house upon the sand:

And the rain descended, and the floods came, and the winds blew, and beat upon that house; and it fell: and great was the fall of it. (Matthew 7: 24-27 KJV)

Focus Questions

1	Name the eight beatitudes.	6	How does Jesus want us to pray?
2	What must you do before making offering to God?	7	Who will enter the Kingdom of heaven?
3	What does Jesus say about adultery?	8	Where does Jesus want us to store our riches?
4	Is divorce recommended by Jesus for any reason?	9	What does Jesus teach about judging others?
5	How should one fast?	10	With what does Jesus compare the person who hears and obeys him?

Note:

In this masterpiece of teaching, Jesus spoke on several topics. His words are just as powerful and relevant today as they were when he spoke them.

Jesus warned, "Enter ye in at the strait gate: for wide is the gate, and broad is the way, that leadeth to destruction, and many there be which go in there at": Matthew 7:13). Tragically, by their search for worldly pleasures and riches, many people today take up the road to destruction. It is vital that they realize their folly sooner or later and take to heart the teachings of Jesus and live a virtuous life to reach their real goal – eternal salvation. When breaking man-made laws, he or she receives a penalty, such as a fine, jail time, or even (depending on the seriousness of the crime and where it occurs) death.

Likewise, when violating the laws of God, he or she may die a Spiritual death and may become separated if not distanced from God.

Reflection

Today divorce and adultery are very prevalent. The teaching of Jesus on these matters is very clear and all are challenged to be obedient to his every word, which does not change with time.

When a person is going through the pain of divorce, Jesus is not asking whose fault it was and he is not holding the sin in front of the person. He wants to heal and set that person free. He wants to take away all the pain, hurt, and emptiness in their lives, if he is approached with repentance and open heart. His grace can break the chains of hatred, jealousy, mistrust and unforgiveness.

Chapter 10
More Parables and Miracles

When Jesus had finished the Sermon on the Mount, he went to Capernaum.

Learning Outcome

- know the circumstances of the miracles in this chapter
- know the message Jesus gives via the parable of the two debtors.

Healing of a Roman Officer's Servant (Miracle 11)

Now when he had ended all his sayings in the audience of the people, he entered into Capernaum.

And a certain centurion's servant, who was dear unto him, was sick, and ready to die.

And when he heard of Jesus, he sent unto him the elders of the Jews, beseeching him that he would come and heal his servant.

And when they came to Jesus, they besought him instantly, saying, that he was worthy for whom he should do this:

For he loveth our nation, and he hath built us a synagogue.

Then Jesus went with them. And when he was now not far from the house, the centurion sent friends to him, saying unto him, Lord, trouble not thyself: for I am not worthy that thou shouldest enter under my roof:

Wherefore neither thought I myself worthy to come unto thee: but say in a word, and my servant shall be healed.

For I also am a man set under authority, having under me soldiers, and I say unto one, Go, and he goeth; and to another, Come, and he cometh; and to my servant, Do this, and he doeth it.

When Jesus heard these things, he marveled at him, and turned him about, and said unto the people that followed him, I say unto you, I have not found so great faith, no, not in Israel.

And they that were sent, returning to the house, found the servant whole that had been sick.

And it came to pass the day after, that he went into a city called Nain; and many of his disciples went with him, and much people.
(Luke 7: 2 - 11 KJV)

Jesus Raises a Widow's Son (Miracle 12)

Now when he came nigh to the gate of the city, behold, there was a dead man carried out, the only son of his mother, and she was a widow: and much people of the city was with her.

And when the Lord saw her, he had compassion on her, and said unto her, Weep not.

And he came and touched the bier: and they that bare him stood still. And he said, Young man, I say unto thee, Arise.

And he that was dead sat up and began to speak. And he delivered him to his mother.

And there came a fear on all: and they glorified God, saying, that a great prophet is risen up among us; and, That God hath visited his people.
(Luke 7: 12-16 KJV)

Jesus at the Home of the Pharisee

And one of the Pharisees desired him that he would eat with him. And he went into the Pharisee's house, and sat down to meat. (Luke 7: 36 KJV)

Sinful Woman Anoints Jesus's Feet

And, behold, a woman in the city, which was a sinner, when she knew that Jesus sat at meat in the Pharisee's house, brought an alabaster box of ointment,

And stood at his feet behind him weeping, and began to wash his feet with tears, and did wipe them with the hairs of her head, and kissed his feet, and anointed them with the ointment.

Now when the Pharisee which had bidden him saw it, he spoke within himself, saying, this man, if he were a prophet, would have known who and what manner of woman this is that toucheth him: for she is a sinner.

And Jesus answering said unto him, Simon, I have somewhat to say unto thee. And he saith, Master, say on. (see below)
(Luke 7: 37-40 KJV)

The Parable of the Two Debtors (Parable 2)

Jesus said to Simon:

There was a certain creditor which had two debtors: the one owed five hundred pence, and the other fifty.

And when they had nothing to pay, he frankly forgave them both. Tell me therefore, which of them will love him most?

Simon answered and said, I suppose that he, to whom he forgave most. And he said unto him, thou hast rightly judged.

And he turned to the woman, and said unto Simon, Seest thou this woman? I entered into thine house, thou gavest me no water for my feet: but she hath washed my feet with tears and wiped them with the hairs of her head.

Thou gavest me no kiss: but this woman since the time I came in hath not ceased to kiss my feet.

My head with oil thou didst not anoint: but this woman hath anointed my feet with ointment.

Wherefore I say unto thee, her sins, which are many, are forgiven; for she loved much: but to whom little is forgiven, the same loveth little.

And he said unto her, thy sins are forgiven.

And they that sat at meat with him began to say within themselves, who is this that forgiveth sins also?

And he said to the woman faith hath saved thee; go in peace. (Luke 7: 41-50 KJV)

In the parable of the two debtors, the forgiving creditor is Jesus, the righteous man owing 50 silver coins is Simon and the sinner owing 500 silver coins is the woman. Simon's lack of concern for Jesus and his little love for him compared to that of the woman show his spiritual bankruptcy. Jesus is willing to forgive Simon but wants him to realize that the woman's loving and faithful attitude is what is required for forgiveness. Jesus can see a desire in the woman to change from her old ways and live a life acceptable to God and so he forgives her sins.

Simon's guests are surprised that Jesus took the divine privilege to forgive the woman's sins.

A parable is a brief story illustrating some lesson or moral. Parables usually have a straight forward meaning and a hidden message.

Sacrifices are Necessary to Follow Jesus

And a certain scribe came, and said unto him, Master, I will follow thee whithersoever thou goest.

And Jesus saith unto him, the foxes have holes, and the birds of the air have nests; but the Son of man hath not where to lay his head.

And another of his disciples said unto him, Lord, suffer me first to go and bury my father.

But Jesus said unto him, follow me; and let the dead bury their dead.
(Matthew 8: 19-22 KJV)

"dead"- those not being called and continue living their life unaware of spiritual things - bury their own dead.

And another also said, Lord, I will follow thee; but let me first go bid them farewell, which are at home at my house.

And Jesus said unto him, no man, having put his hand to the plough, and looking back, is fit for the kingdom of God.
(Luke 9: 61-62 KJV)

He further said:

For which of you, intending to build a tower, sitteth not down first, and counteth the cost, whether he have sufficient to finish it?

Lest haply, after he hath laid the foundation, and is not able to finish it, all that behold it begin to mock him,

Saying, this man began to build, and was not able to finish.

Or what king, going to make war against another king, sitteth not down first, and consulteth whether he be able with ten thousand to meet him that cometh against him with twenty thousand?

Or else, while the other is yet a great way off, he sendeth an ambassage, and desireth conditions of peace.

So likewise, whosoever he be of you that forsaketh not all that he hath, he cannot be my disciple.
(Luke 14: 28-33 KJV)

A Blind and Dumb Man Gets Healed (Miracle 13)

Then was brought unto him one possessed with a devil, blind, and dumb: and he healed him, insomuch that the blind and dumb both spoke and saw.
(Matthew 12: 22 KJV)

Pharisees Say Beelzebul Gives Jesus the Power

But when the Pharisees heard it, they said, this fellow doth not cast out devils, but by Beelzebub the prince of the devils.

And Jesus knew their thoughts, and said unto them, every kingdom divided against itself is brought to desolation; and every city or house divided against itself shall not stand:

And if Satan cast out Satan, he is divided against himself; how shall then his kingdom stand?

And if I by Beelzebub cast out devils, by whom do your children cast them out? therefore they shall be your judges.

But if I cast out devils by the Spirit of God, then the kingdom of God is come unto you.

Or else how can one enter into a strong man's house, and spoil his goods, except he first bind the strong man? and then he will spoil his house.

He that is not with me is against me; and he that gathereth not with me scattereth abroad.

Wherefore I say unto you, all manner of sin and blasphemy shall be forgiven unto men: but the blasphemy against the Holy Ghost shall not be forgiven unto men.

And whosoever speaketh a word against the Son of man, it shall be forgiven him: but whosoever speaketh against the Holy Ghost, it shall not be forgiven him, neither in this world, neither in the world to come.

Either make the tree good, and his fruit good; or else make the tree corrupt, and his fruit corrupt: for the tree is known by his fruit.

O generation of vipers, how can ye, being evil, speak good things? for out of the abundance of the heart the mouth speaketh.

A good man out of the good treasure of the heart bringeth forth good things: and an evil man out of the evil treasure bringeth forth evil things.

But I say unto you, that every idle word that men shall speak, they shall give account thereof in the day of judgment.

For by thy words thou shalt be justified, and by thy words thou shalt be condemned.
(Matthew 12: 24-37 KJV)

Jesus's Mother and Brothers

While he yet talked to the people, behold, his mother and his brethren stood without, desiring to speak with him.

Then one said unto him, Behold, thy mother and thy brethren stand without, desiring to speak with thee.

But he answered and said unto him that told him, who is my mother? and who are my brethren?

And he stretched forth his hand toward his disciples, and said, Behold my mother and my brethren!

For whosoever shall do the will of my Father which is in heaven, the same is my brother, and sister, and mother.
(Matthew 12: 46-50 KJV)

Focus Questions

1	What are parables?	5	What connection did Jesus demonstrate between one's love for him and the forgiveness he gives?
2	What lesson can we learn from the parable of the two debtors?	6	What did Jesus mean when he said, "Let the dead bury the dead"?
3	Who did Jesus say his mother and brothers and sisters were?	7	What did Jesus say about someone speaking something against the Holy Spirit?
4	Who did Jesus say gives him power to drive out demons?	8	Who did Jesus say can be his disciples?

Note:

The most common way Jesus taught us was through parables. His parables appealed to the young and old, poor and rich, and to the learned and unlearned as well. His parables are like buried treasure waiting to be discovered.

While his parables are rooted in a specific time and place, they nonetheless speak of timeless realities to people of every time and place. They underline the fact that God works in every age and he meets us in the ordinary and everyday situations of life.

Each parable of Jesus has a literal meaning, apparent to anyone who has experience with the subject matter. But beyond the literal meaning lies a deeper meaning, a beneath-the-surface lesson about God's truth and his kingdom.

For example, the parable "the simple transformation of dough into bread by the inclusion of the yeast" is likened to, God transforming us when we allow his word and Spirit to take root in our hearts.

Jesus told his disciples that not everyone would understand his parables. 'To you it has been given to know the secrets of the kingdom of God; but for others they are in parables, so that seeing they may not see, and hearing they may not hear.'

The parables of Jesus will enlighten us only if we approach them with an open mind and heart, ready to let them challenge us. If we approach them with the conviction that we already know the answer, then we, too, may look but not see, listen but not hear or understand. When reading the parables, it is important to not get bogged down in the details of the story. The main learning is in the concept.

Reflection

To hear the words of Jesus is an activity of our God-given intellect alone, but to let his words pierce us and change us calls for openness to the Holy Spirit and a willingness to be changed.

Chapter 11
The Kingdom of Heaven

Jesus explains the nature of the Kingdom of heaven using parables.

Learning Outcome

- understand the parables concerning the Kingdom of Heaven

The Parable of the Sower (Parable 3)

The same day went Jesus out of the house and sat by the sea side.

And great multitudes were gathered together unto him, so that he went into a ship, and sat; and the whole multitude stood on the shore.

And he spoke many things unto them in parables, saying, Behold, a sower went forth to sow;

And when he sowed, some seeds fell by the way side, and the fowls came and devoured them up:

Some fell upon stony places, where they had not much earth: and forthwith they sprung up, because they had no deepness of earth:

And when the sun was up, they were scorched; and because they had no root, they withered away.

And some fell among thorns; and the thorns sprung up, and choked them:

But other fell into good ground, and brought forth fruit, some an hundredfold, some sixtyfold, some thirtyfold.

Who hath ears to hear, let him hear.

The Purpose of Parables

And the disciples came, and said unto him, Why speakest thou unto them in parables?

He answered and said unto them, because it is given unto you to know the mysteries of the kingdom of heaven, but to them it is not given.

For whosoever hath, to him shall be given, and he shall have more abundance: but whosoever hath not, from him shall be taken away even that he hath.

Therefore, speak I to them in parables: because they seeing see not; and hearing they hear not, neither do they understand.
(Matthew 13: 1-13 KJV)

But blessed are your eyes, for they see: and your ears, for they hear.

For verily I say unto you, that many prophets and righteous men have desired to see those things which ye see and have not seen them; and to hear those things which ye hear and have not heard them.
(Matthew 13: 16-17 KJV)

What the parable of the sower means is this:

Those who hear the message about the Kingdom but do not understand it are like the seeds that fell along the path. The Evil One comes and snatches away what was sown in them.

The seeds that fell on rocky ground stand for those who receive the message gladly as soon as they hear it. But it does not sink deep into them, and they don't last long. So, when trouble or persecution comes because of the message, they give up at once.

The seeds that fell among thorn bushes stand for those who hear the message; but the worries about this life and the love for riches choke the message; and they don't bear fruit.

And the seeds sown in the good soil stand for those who hear the message and understand it; they bear fruit, some as much as one hundred, others sixty, and others thirty."

The Light of the Body

No man, when he hath lighted a candle, putteth it in a secret place, neither under a bushel, but on a candlestick, that they which come in may see the light.

The light of the body is the eye: therefore, when thine eye is single, thy whole body also is full of light; but when thine eye is evil, thy body also is full of darkness.

Take heed therefore that the light which is in thee be not darkness.

If thy whole body therefore be full of light, having no part dark, the whole shall be full of light, as when the bright shining of a candle doth give thee light.
(Luke 11: 33-36 KJV)

The Parable of the Growing Seed (Parable 4)

And he said, so is the kingdom of God, as if a man should cast seed into the ground;

And should sleep, and rise night and day, and the seed should spring and grow up, he knoweth not how.

For the earth bringeth forth fruit of herself; first the blade, then the ear, after that the full corn in the ear.

But when the fruit is brought forth, immediately he putteth in the sickle, because the harvest is come.
(Mark 4: 26 – 29 KJV)

Once the seed, the word of God, is sown in one's heart (the field), it grows into convictions and applications (fruits & grains) which make one's faith (harvest) of a quality acceptable to God for salvation. God himself works behind the scenes doing most of the work.

The Parable of the Weeds (Parable 5)

Another parable put he forth unto them, saying, the kingdom of heaven is likened unto a man which sowed good seed in his field:

But while men slept, his enemy came and sowed tares among the wheat, and went his way.

But when the blade was sprung up, and brought forth fruit, then appeared the tares also.

So, the servants of the householder came and said unto him, Sir, didst not thou sow good seed in thy field? from whence then hath it tears?

He said unto them, an enemy hath done this. The servants said unto him, wilt thou then that we go and gather them up?

But he said, Nay; lest while ye gather up the tares, ye root up also the wheat with them.

Let both grow together until the harvest: and in the time of harvest I will say to the reapers, gather ye together first the tares, and bind them in bundles to burn them: but gather the wheat into my barn.
(Matthew 13: 24-30 KJV)

The man who sowed the good seed is the Son of Man; the field is the world; the good seed is the people who belong to the Kingdom; the weeds are the people who belong to the Evil One; and the enemy who sowed the weed is the Devil. The harvest is the end of the age and the harvest workers are the angels. Just as the weeds are gathered up and burned in the fire, so the same thing will happen at the end of the age: the Son of Man will send out his angels to gather up out of his Kingdom all those who cause people to sin and all others who do evil things, and they will throw them into the fiery furnace, where they will cry and gnash their teeth. Then the God's people will shine like the sun in their Father's Kingdom.

The Parable of the Mustard Seed (Parable 6)

Another parable put he forth unto them, saying, the kingdom of heaven is like to a grain of mustard seed, which a man took, and sowed in his field:

Which indeed is the least of all seeds: but when it is grown, it is the greatest among herbs, and becometh a tree, so that the birds of the air come and lodge in the branches thereof.
(Matthew 13: 31-32 KJV)

The sower is Jesus. The mustard seed represents the word of God. The field is the world. The Word grows to reach millions of people. It offers the faithful a refuge in Jesus.

The Parable of the Yeast (Parable 7)

Another parable spoke he unto them; The kingdom of heaven is like unto leaven, which a woman took, and hid in three measures of meal, till the whole was leavened.
(Matthew 13: 33 KJV)

Parable of the Yeast has similar, yet a different meaning, to the Parable of the Mustard Seed; it refers to the Word of God leavening the world and gracing the believer.

The Parable of the Hidden Treasure (Parable 8)

Again, the kingdom of heaven is like unto treasure hid in a field; which when a man hath found, he hideth, and for joy thereof goeth and selleth all that he hath, and buyeth that field.
(Matthew 13: 44 KJV)

The kingdom here refers to God's rule on earth and is likened to a treasure. The parable describes its value to one who accidentally finds it. The one who finds it must assume the responsibility to share it with others.

The Parable of the Pearl (Parable 9)

Again, the kingdom of heaven is like unto a merchant man, seeking goodly pearls:

Who, when he had found one pearl of great price, went and sold all that he had, and bought it.
(Matthew 13: 45-46 KJV)

The parable of the pearl appears similar to the parable of the treasure. However, there is a subtle difference. Treasure is a mixture of precious things while the pearl is a single precious thing representing different aspects of the costliness and the joy they give to the purchaser.

The Parable of the Net (Parable 10)

Again, the kingdom of heaven is like unto a net, that was cast into the sea, and gathered of every kind:

Which, when it was full, they drew to shore, and sat down, and gathered the good into vessels, but cast the bad away.

So shall it be at the end of the world: the angels shall come forth, and sever the wicked from among the just,

And shall cast them into the furnace of fire: there shall be wailing and gnashing of teeth.

Jesus saith unto them, have ye understood all these things? They say unto him, Yea, Lord.

Then said he unto them, therefore every scribe which is instructed unto the kingdom of heaven is like unto a man that is an householder, which bringeth forth out of his treasure things new and old.
(Matthew 13: 47-52 KJV)

The important message from this parable is that everyone will be judged at the end, and so it is wise to follow what the Gospel teaches. The righteous people will be separated from the wicked people.

Focus Questions

1	Why did Jesus speak in Parables?	4	To what did Jesus liken the Kingdom of Heaven?
2	Distinguish between the parable of the treasure and the parable of the pearl.	5	What is the message Jesus gives through the parable of the sower?
3	What can be learned from the parable of the net?	6	How does the parable of the yeast differ from the parable of the mustard seed?

Note:

The numerous parables about the kingdom of heaven provide us with good analogies that are meant to help us understand the value of God's Kingdom. The clear message is that no matter how much earthly wealth one has, the Kingdom of Heaven is worth far more to us and it is worthwhile giving up everything we have in the pursuit of spiritual happiness. While this seems a bold claim, if we look closely at our own life, we will find that the moments of true inner peace and happiness were felt after acts of selfless love.

By building up our lives on the word of God we are filling ourselves with true happiness and peace. Then God's kingdom, his spiritual reign, is within us.

Reflection

We are transformed by God's kingdom when we allow his words to take root in our hearts. After transformation we are to be leaven that transforms the society in which we live and work. (that is, we must be like the yeast that ferments the dough)

Chapter 12
Five More Miracles

Jesus performs variety of miracles.

Learning Outcome

* Know the circumstances of each miracle in this chapter

Jesus Calms a Storm (Miracle 14)

Now it came to pass on a certain day, that he went into a ship with his disciples: and he said unto them, let us go over unto the other side of the lake. And they launched forth.

But as they sailed, he fell asleep: and there came down a storm of wind on the lake; and they were filled with water and were in jeopardy.

And they came to him, and awoke him, saying, Master, master, we perish. Then he arose and rebuked the wind and the raging of the water: and they ceased, and there was a calm.

And he said unto them, where is your faith? And they being afraid wondered, saying one to another, What manner of man is this! for he commandeth even the winds and water, and they obey him.
(Luke 8: 22-25 KJV)

By calming the storm Jesus demonstrated his control over Nature.

Jesus Sends the Demons into Pigs (Miracle 15)

And they arrived at the country of the Gadarenes, which is over against Galilee.

And when he went forth to land, there met him out of the city a certain man, which had devils long time, and ware no clothes, neither abode in any house, but in the tombs.

When he saw Jesus, he cried out, and fell down before him, and with a loud voice said, what have I to do with thee, Jesus, thou Son of God most high? I beseech thee, torment me not.
(For he had commanded the unclean spirit to come out of the man. For oftentimes it had caught him: and he was kept bound with chains and in fetters; and he brake the bands and was driven of the devil into the wilderness.)

And Jesus asked him, saying, what is thy name? And he said, Legion: because many devils were entered into him.

And they besought him that he would not command them to go out into the deep.

And there was there an herd of many swine feeding on the mountain: and they besought him that he would suffer them to enter into them. And he suffered them.

Then went the devils out of the man and entered into the swine: and the herd ran violently down a steep place into the lake and were choked.

When they that fed them saw what was done, they fled, and went and told it in the city and in the country.

Then they went out to see what was done; and came to Jesus, and found the man, out of whom the devils were departed, sitting at the feet of Jesus, clothed, and in his right mind: and they were afraid.

They also which saw it told them by what means he that was possessed of the devils was healed.

Then the whole multitude of the country of the Gadarenes round about besought him to depart from them; for they were taken with great fear: and he went up into the ship and returned back again.

Now the man out of whom the devils were departed besought him that he might be with him: but Jesus sent him away, saying,

Return to thine own house and shew how great things God hath done unto thee. And he went his way and published throughout the whole city how great things Jesus had done unto him.
(Luke 8: 26-39 KJV)

Jesus Cures a Woman in the Crowd (Miracle 16)

Jesus Cures Jairus' Daughter (Miracle 17)

And, behold, there came a man named Jairus, and he was a ruler of the synagogue: and he fell down at Jesus' feet, and besought him that he would come into his house:

For he had one only daughter, about twelve years of age, and she lay a dying. But as he went the people thronged him.

And a woman having an issue of blood twelve years, which had spent all her living upon physicians, neither could be healed of any,

Came behind him and touched the border of his garment: and immediately her issue of blood stanched.

And Jesus said, who touched me? When all denied, Peter and they that were with him said, Master, the multitude throng thee and press thee, and sayest thou, who touched me?

And Jesus said, somebody hath touched me: for I perceive that virtue is gone out of me.

And when the woman saw that she was not hid, she came trembling, and falling down before him, she declared unto him before all the people for what cause she had touched him, and how she was healed immediately.

And he said unto her, Daughter, be of good comfort: thy faith hath made thee whole; go in peace.

While he yet spoke, there cometh one from the ruler of the synagogue's house, saying to him, thy daughter is dead; trouble not the Master.

But when Jesus heard it, he answered him, saying, Fear not: believe only, and she shall be made whole.

And when he came into the house, he suffered no man to go in, save Peter, and James, and John, and the father and the mother of the maiden.

And all wept, and bewailed her: but he said, Weep not; she is not dead, but sleepeth.

And they laughed him to scorn, knowing that she was dead.

And he put them all out, and took her by the hand, and called, saying, Maid, arise.

And her spirit came again, and she arose straightway: and he commanded to give her meat.

And her parents were astonished: but he charged them that they should tell no man what was done.
(Luke 8: 41-56 KJV)

Jesus Heals Two Blind Men (Miracle 18)

And when Jesus departed thence, two blind men followed him, crying, and saying, thou son of David, have mercy on us.

And when he was come into the house, the blind men came to him: and Jesus saith unto them, believe ye that I am able to do this? They said unto him, Yea, Lord.

Then touched he their eyes, saying, according to your faith be it unto you.

And their eyes were opened; and Jesus straitly charged them, saying, see that no man know it.
(Matthew 9: 27-30 KJV)

By restoring the eye sight Jesus demonstrated that he is the "light of the world" He tells not to tell anyone about his miracle because if they did, he could no longer enter a town openly.

Focus Questions

1	After performing a miracle why did Jesus sometimes ask not to tell anyone?	2	Even when Jesus was by their side, the apostles were afraid of disasters? Why is that?

Note:

The miracles that are documented in the Bible demonstrate the power of Jesus derived from God over all things that affect humanity. Jesus repeatedly asks people for one thing, to believe in his ability to achieve the miraculous outcomes that people were asking of him. This expectation is no different today, but is significantly more difficult because the outcome, although sometimes miraculous, is not often direct and clear in answer to a specific request. Beliefs in 'miracles' does not seem common in today's society. This may be due to our inability to recognize them for what they are, because sometimes they contrast with our expectations. (often God has a plan different to ours)

One thing is clear however, if we do not believe in the possibility of miracles, what right do we have to expect our problems to be solved 'miraculously' when we ask out of desperation in our time of greatest need?

Reflection

The story of the woman with hemorrhage drives home to us the fact that Jesus can even heal without being asked. The woman didn't ask but instead reached out to Jesus by faith, and she was healed.

His raising of Jairus' daughter is an example of Jesus' power even over death.

How can his power over disease, forces of nature and death not evoke in us a faith in him?

As a compassionate and powerful God, would he not reach out to the neediest of human beings who cry out for help from him?

Chapter 13
Jesus in Synagogue - Apostles Given Powers

Jesus shows his authority as God.

Learning Outcome

- know a scripture Jesus explained in the Synagogue
- know the powers Jesus gave his apostles

Jesus in Synagogue

And he came to Nazareth, where he had been brought up: and, as his custom was, he went into the synagogue on the sabbath day, and stood up to read.

And there was delivered unto him the book of the prophet Esaias. And when he had opened the book, he found the place where it was written,

The Spirit of the Lord is upon me, because he hath anointed me to preach the gospel to the poor; he hath sent me to heal the broken-hearted, to preach deliverance to the captives, and recovering of sight to the blind, to set at liberty them that are bruised,

To preach the acceptable year of the Lord.

And he closed the book, and he gave it again to the minister, and sat down. And the eyes of all them that were in the synagogue were fastened on him. And he began to say unto them, this day is this scripture fulfilled in your ears.

And all bare him witness and wondered at the gracious words which proceeded out of his mouth. And they said, Is not this Joseph's son?

And he said unto them, Ye will surely say unto me this proverb, Physician, heal thyself: whatsoever we have heard done in Capernaum, do also here in thy country.

And he said, Verily I say unto you, no prophet is accepted in his own country.

But I tell you of a truth, many widows were in Israel in the days of Elias, when the heaven was shut up three years and six months, when great famine was throughout all the land;

But unto none of them was Elias sent, save unto Sarepta, a city of Sidon, unto a woman that was a widow.

And many lepers were in Israel in the time of Eliseus the prophet; and none of them was cleansed, saving Naaman the Syrian.

And all they in the synagogue, when they heard these things, were filled with wrath,

And rose up, and thrust him out of the city, and led him unto the brow of the hill whereon their city was built, that they might cast him down headlong.

But he passing through the midst of them went his way,
(Luke 4: 16-30 KJV)

And Jesus went about all the cities and villages, teaching in their synagogues, and preaching the gospel of the kingdom, and healing every sickness and every disease among the people.

But when he saw the multitudes, he was moved with compassion on them, because they fainted, and were scattered abroad, as sheep having no shepherd.

Then saith he unto his disciples, the harvest truly is plenteous, but the laborers are few;

Pray ye therefore the Lord of the harvest, that he will send forth laborers into his harvest.
(Matthew 9: 35-38 KJV)

The harvest represents the people who are longing to hear the Word of God. The workers are the people who spread the Word.

Jesus Gives Authority to Apostles

Then he called his twelve disciples together, and gave them power and authority over all devils, and to cure diseases.
(Luke 9: 1 KJV)

These twelve Jesus sent forth, and commanded them, saying, Go not into the way of the Gentiles, and into any city of the Samaritans enter ye not:

But go rather to the lost sheep of the house of Israel.

And as ye go, preach, saying, the kingdom of heaven is at hand.

Heal the sick, cleanse the lepers, raise the dead, cast out devils: freely ye have received, freely give.

Provide neither gold, nor silver, nor brass in your purses,

Nor scrip for your journey, neither two coats, neither shoes, nor yet staves: for the workman is worthy of his meat.

And into whatsoever city or town ye shall enter, enquire who in it is worthy; and there abide till ye go thence.

And when ye come into an house, salute it.

And if the house be worthy, let your peace come upon it: but if it be not worthy, let your peace return to you.

And whosoever shall not receive you, nor hear your words, when ye depart out of that house or city, shake off the dust of your feet.

Verily I say unto you, It shall be more tolerable for the land of Sodom and Gomorrah in the day of judgment, than for that city.

Behold, I send you forth as sheep in the midst of wolves: be ye therefore wise as serpents, and harmless as doves.

But beware of men: for they will deliver you up to the councils, and they will scourge you in their synagogues;

And ye shall be brought before governors and kings for my sake, for a testimony against them and the Gentiles.

But when they deliver you up, take no thought how or what ye shall speak: for it shall be given you in that same hour what ye shall speak.

For it is not ye that speak, but the Spirit of your Father which speaketh in you.

And the brother shall deliver up the brother to death, and the father the child: and the children shall rise up against their parents and cause them to be put to death.

And ye shall be hated of all men for my name's sake: but he that endured to the end shall be saved.

But when they persecute you in this city, flee ye into another: for verily I say unto you, Ye shall not have gone over the cities of Israel, till the Son of man be come.

The disciple is not above his master, nor the servant above his lord.

It is enough for the disciple that he be as his master, and the servant as his lord. If they have called the master of the house Beelzebub, how much more shall they call them of his household?

Fear them not therefore: for there is nothing covered, that shall not be revealed; and hid, that shall not be known.

What I tell you in darkness, that speak ye in light: and what ye hear in the ear, that preach ye upon the housetops.

And fear not them which kill the body but are not able to kill the soul: but rather fear him which is able to destroy both soul and body in hell.

Are not two sparrows sold for a farthing? and one of them shall not fall on the ground without your Father.

But the very hairs of your head are all numbered.

Fear ye not therefore, ye are of more value than many sparrows.

Whosoever therefore shall confess me before men, him will I confess also before my Father which is in heaven.

But whosoever shall deny me before men, him will I also deny before my Father which is in heaven.

Think not that I am come to send peace on earth: I came not to send peace, but a sword.

For I am come to set a man at variance against his father, and the daughter against her mother, and the daughter in law against her mother in law.

And a man's foes shall be they of his own household.

He that loveth father or mother more than me is not worthy of me: and he that loveth son or daughter more than me is not worthy of me.

And he that taketh not his cross, and followeth after me, is not worthy of me.

He that findeth his life shall lose it: and he that loseth his life for my sake shall find it.

He that receiveth you receiveth me, and he that receiveth me receiveth him that sent me.
(Matthew 10: 5-40 KJV)

Ye are the salt of the earth: but if the salt have lost his savor, wherewith shall it be salted? it is thenceforth good for nothing, but to be cast out, and to be trodden under foot of men.
(Matthew 5: 13 KJV)

After these things the Lord appointed other seventy also and sent them two and two before his face into every city and place, whither he himself would come.
(Luke 10: 1 KJV)

Focus Questions

1	What eloquent words of Jesus impressed the people in the synagogue?	4	What authority did Jesus give to the apostles?
2	What did Jesus say in the synagogue to upset the people?	5	What instructions did Jesus give the apostles when he sent them out to spread the Kingdom of God?
3	What did Jesus mean when he said, "the harvest is large but there are few workers to gather it."?	6	Summarize the instructions Jesus gave his apostles when he sent them out to spread the Good News?

Note:

Jesus predicted the hardships to be faced by anyone spreading His words, because the truth is painful and difficult to hear. Most attack the truth rather than accept it. Those who preach the truth find themselves banging their heads against brick walls. The truth does not bring about peace but instead it brings anger and dissention. Jesus preached peace and love but faced anger, bitterness, attacks and blasphemies.

What is it about humans that makes them reject true messages, even when the messages are so clearly innocent and meant for their own benefit?

Reflection

We cannot hear God's message when the world is shouting in our ears! We need to focus our thoughts to hear God's silent voice. It may well be a meditation to invite God to speak to us.

Chapter 14
Jesus's Unusual Miracles

Two unusual miracles Jesus performed are given in this chapter.

Learning Outcome

• know two unusual miracles that Jesus performed

Jesus Feeds Five Thousand (Miracle 19)

And the apostles gathered themselves together unto Jesus, and told him all things, both what they had done, and what they had taught.

And he said unto them, come ye yourselves apart into a desert place, and rest a while: for there were many coming and going, and they had no leisure so much as to eat.

And they departed into a desert place by ship privately.

And the people saw them departing, and many knew him, and ran afoot thither out of all cities, and outwent them, and came together unto him.

And Jesus, when he came out, saw much people, and was moved with compassion toward them, because they were as sheep not having a shepherd: and he began to teach them many things.
(Mark 6: 30-34 KJV)

And when it was evening, his disciples came to him, saying, this is a desert place, and the time is now past; send the multitude away, that they may go into the villages, and buy themselves victuals.

But Jesus said unto them, they need not depart; give ye them to eat.

And they say unto him, we have here but five loaves, and two fishes.

He said, Bring them hither to me.

And he commanded the multitude to sit down on the grass, and took the five loaves, and the two fishes, and looking up to heaven, he blessed, and broke, and gave the loaves to his disciples, and the disciples to the multitude.

And they did all eat and were filled: and they took up of the fragments that remained twelve baskets full.

And they that had eaten were about five thousand men, beside women and children.
(Matthew 14: 15-21 KJV)

When they were filled, he said unto his disciples, gather up the fragments that remain, that nothing be lost.
(John 6: 12 KJV)

Jesus Walks on the Water (Miracle 20)

And straightway Jesus constrained his disciples to get into a ship, and to go before him unto the other side, while he sent the multitudes away.

And when he had sent the multitudes away, he went up into a mountain apart to pray: and when the evening was come, he was there alone.

But the ship was now in the midst of the sea, tossed with waves: for the wind was contrary.

And in the fourth watch of the night Jesus went unto them, walking on the sea.

And when the disciples saw him walking on the sea, they were troubled, saying, it is a spirit; and they cried out for fear.

But straightway Jesus spoke unto them, saying, be of good cheer; it is I; be not afraid.

And Peter answered him and said, Lord, if it be thou, bid me come unto thee on the water.

And he said, Come. And when Peter was come down out of the ship, he walked on the water, to go to Jesus.

But when he saw the wind boisterous, he was afraid; and beginning to sink, he cried, saying, Lord, save me.

And immediately Jesus stretched forth his hand, and caught him, and said unto him, O thou of little faith, wherefore didst thou doubt?

And when they were come into the ship, the wind ceased.

Then they that were in the ship came and worshipped him, saying, Of a truth thou art the Son of God.
(Matthew 14: 22-33 KJV)

The Healing at the Pool (Miracle 21)

After this there was a feast of the Jews; and Jesus went up to Jerusalem.

Now there is at Jerusalem by the sheep market a pool, which is called in the Hebrew tongue Bethesda, having five porches.

In these lay a great multitude of impotent folk, of blind, halt, withered, waiting for the moving of the water.

For an angel went down at a certain season into the pool, and troubled the water: whosoever then first after the troubling of the water stepped in was made whole of whatsoever disease he had.

And a certain man was there, which had an infirmity* thirty and eight years.

When Jesus saw him lie, and knew that he had been now a long time in that case, he saith unto him, Wilt thou be made whole?

The impotent man answered him, Sir, I have no man, when the water is troubled, to put me into the pool: but while* I am coming, another steppeth down before me.

Jesus saith unto him, Rise, take up thy bed, and walk.

And immediately the man was made whole, and took up his bed, and walked: and on the same day was the sabbath.

The Jews therefore said unto him that was cured, It is the sabbath day: it is not lawful for thee to carry thy bed.

He answered them, He that made me whole, the same said unto me, Take up thy bed, and walk.

Then asked they him, What man is that which said unto thee, Take up thy bed, and walk?

And he that was healed wist not who it was: for Jesus had conveyed himself away, a multitude being in that place.

Afterward* Jesus findeth him in the temple, and said unto him, Behold, thou art made whole: sin no more, lest a worse thing* come unto thee.

The man departed, and told the Jews that it was Jesus, which had made him whole.
(John 5: 1-15 KJV)

Focus Questions

1	How many baskets of food were left after feeding the five thousand people?	2	What did Jesus say to Peter when he cried out 'save me Lord,' despite Jesus saying, 'don't be afraid'?

Note:

Jesus said: 'Stop sinning, otherwise worse things may happen to you". The inference here may appear to be that human sufferings are the result of sins committed. Do sins bring tragedies? Can a loving and compassionate God allow that? Perhaps it is being cruel to be kind, an example of what our society today calls "tough love".

Reflection

"Even when everything crumbles around us and perhaps even in us, Jesus remains our unfailing support" - **Pope John Paul**.

Chapter 15
More Parables and Miracles

Jesus narrates more parables and performs more miracles

Learning Outcome

- know what makes a person unclean
- know what Jesus meant by 'the yeast' of the Pharisees and Sadducees

Disobeying God's Commands

Then came to Jesus scribes and Pharisees, which were of Jerusalem, saying,

Why do thy disciples transgress the tradition of the elders? for they wash not their hands when they eat bread.

But he answered and said unto them, why do ye also transgress the commandment of God by your tradition?

For God commanded, saying, honour thy father and mother: and, He that curseth father or mother, let him die the death.

But ye say, whosoever shall say to his father or his mother, It is a gift, by whatsoever thou mightest be profited by me;

And honour not his father or his mother, he shall be free. Thus, have ye made the commandment of God of none effect by your tradition.

Ye hypocrites, well did Esaias prophesy of you, saying,

This people draweth nigh unto me with their mouth, and honoureth me
with their lips; but their heart is far from me.
(Matthew 15: 1 – 8 KJV)

Things that Make a Person Unclean

And he called the multitude, and said unto them, Hear, and understand:

Not that which goeth into the mouth defileth a man; but that which
cometh out of the mouth, this defileth a man.

Then came his disciples, and said unto him, knowest thou that the
Pharisees were offended, after they heard this saying?

But he answered and said, every plant, which my heavenly Father hath
not planted, shall be rooted up.

Let them alone: they be blind leaders of the blind. And if the blind lead
the blind, both shall fall into the ditch.

Then answered Peter and said unto him, Declare unto us this parable.

And Jesus said, are ye also yet without understanding?

Do not ye yet understand, that whatsoever entereth in at the mouth goeth
into the belly, and is cast out into the draught?

But those things which proceed out of the mouth come forth from the
heart; and they defile the man.

For out of the heart proceed evil thoughts, murders, adulteries, fornications,
thefts, false witness, blasphemies:

These are the things which defile a man: but to eat with unwashen hands defileth not a man.
(Matthew 15: 10 – 20 KJV)

Canaanite Woman's Daughter Healed (Miracle 22)

Then Jesus went thence, and departed into the coasts of Tyre and Sidon.

And, behold, a woman of Canaan came out of the same coasts, and cried unto him, saying, have mercy on me, O Lord, thou son of David; my daughter is grievously vexed with a devil.

But he answered her not a word. And his disciples came and besought him, saying, Send her away; for she crieth after us.

But he answered and said, I am not sent but unto the lost sheep of the house of Israel.

Then came she and worshipped him, saying, Lord, help me.

But he answered and said, it is not meet to take the children's bread, and to cast it to dogs.

And she said, Truth, Lord: yet the dogs eat of the crumbs which fall from their master's table.

Then Jesus answered and said unto her, O woman, great is thy faith: be it unto thee even as thou wilt. And her daughter was made whole from that very hour.
(Matthew 15: 21 - 28 KJV)

Jesus Heals a Deaf - Mute (Miracle 23)

And again, departing from the coasts of Tyre and Sidon, he came unto the sea of Galilee, through the midst of the coasts of Decapolis.

And they bring unto him one that was deaf and had an impediment in his speech; and they beseech him to put his hand upon him.

And he took him aside from the multitude, and put his fingers into his ears, and he spit, and touched his tongue;

And looking up to heaven, he sighed, and saith unto him, Ephphatha, that is, be opened.

And straightway his ears were opened, and the string of his tongue was loosed, and he spoke plain.
(Mark 7: 31 - 35 KJV)

Jesus Feeds Four Thousand (Miracle 24)

Then Jesus called his disciples unto him, and said, I have compassion on the multitude, because they continue with me now three days, and have nothing to eat: and I will not send them away fasting, lest they faint in the way.

And his disciples say unto him, whence should we have so much bread in the wilderness, as to fill so great a multitude?

And Jesus saith unto them, how many loaves have ye? And they said, Seven, and a few little fishes.

And he commanded the multitude to sit down on the ground.

And he took the seven loaves and the fishes, and gave thanks, and broke them, and gave to his disciples, and the disciples to the multitude.

And they did all eat and were filled: and they took up of the broken meat that was left seven baskets full.

And they that did eat were four thousand men, beside women and children.
(Matthew 15: 32 - 38 KJV)

Yeast of the Pharisees And Sadducees (Parable 11)

And when his disciples were come to the other side, they had forgotten to take bread.

Then Jesus said unto them, take heed and beware of the leaven of the Pharisees and of the Sadducees.

And they reasoned among themselves, saying, It is because we have taken no bread.

Which when Jesus perceived, he said unto them, O ye of little faith, why reason ye among yourselves, because ye have brought no bread?

Do ye not yet understand, neither remember the five loaves of the five thousand, and how many baskets ye took up?

Neither the seven loaves of the four thousand, and how many baskets ye took up?

How is it that ye do not understand that I spoke it not to you concerning bread, that ye should beware of the leaven of the Pharisees and of the Sadducees?

Then understood they how that he bade them not beware of the leaven of bread, but of the doctrine of the Pharisees and of the Sadducees. (Matthew 16: 5 - 12 KJV)

Jesus Heals a Blind Man at Bethsaida (miracle 25)

And he cometh to Bethsaida; and they bring a blind man unto him and besought him to touch him.

And he took the blind man by the hand and led him out of the town; and when he had spit on his eyes, and put his hands upon him, he asked him if he saw ought.

And he looked up, and said, I see men as trees, walking.

After that he put his hands again upon his eyes and made him look up: and he was restored and saw every man clearly. (Mark 8: 22 – 25 KJV)

Focus Questions

1	What things make a person unclean according to Jesus?	3	What did Jesus mean when he said 'guard yourselves from the yeast of the Pharisees and Sadducees?
2	What was the Canaanite woman's reply when Jesus told her 'it is not right to take the children's food and throw it to the dogs?		

Note:

The desire for healing is good, especially when it takes the form of prayer. Prayer is not merely the repetition of certain words, but a sincere communication uttered on the basis of faith. A prayer is more than a simple request for help, it is an acknowledgment of the need for God's assistance and an expression of desire to conform to and accept His will. Prayer does not necessarily result in a specific outcome that might have been envisioned when the prayer was uttered; the effect is that which God only knows and understands as the right response to the prayerful request. The desire for healing is one of the fundamental characteristics of human experience, and prayer is one of the responses to that desire. (Pope Benedict XVI)

Reflection

At times we may feel that God seems to be letting us down, but we need to remember the abundance of goodness of God we have previously enjoyed! We who are happy to receive good things from God must be prepared to accept bad things as well because he gives them to us out of a desire to teach us, his loving children. He sees our strengths and weaknesses and is committed to teaching and leading us to the final promised land of heaven.

Chapter 16
Transfiguration of Jesus

Jesus shows his association with heaven.

Learning Outcome

- know the significance of the transfiguration of Jesus
- know what Jesus said one must do to be his disciple

Peter's Declaration about Jesus

When Jesus came into the coasts of Caesarea Philippi, he asked his disciples, saying, whom do men say that I the Son of man am?

And they said, some say that thou art John the Baptist: some, Elias; and others, Jeremias, or one of the prophets.

He saith unto them, but whom say ye that I am?

And Simon Peter answered and said, Thou art the Christ, the Son of the living God.

And Jesus answered and said unto him, Blessed art thou, Simon Barjona: for flesh and blood hath not revealed it unto thee, but my Father which is in heaven.

And I say also unto thee, that thou art Peter, and upon this rock I will build my church; and the gates of hell shall not prevail against it.

And I will give unto thee the keys of the kingdom of heaven: and whatsoever thou shalt bind on earth shall be bound in heaven: and whatsoever thou shalt loose on earth shall be loosed in heaven. (Matthew 16: 13 – 19 KJV)

Jesus Speaks about His Death for the First Time

And he began to teach them, that the Son of man must suffer many things, and be rejected of the elders, and of the chief priests, and scribes, and be killed, and after three days rise again.

And he spoke that saying openly. And Peter took him and began to rebuke him.

But when he had turned about and looked on his disciples, he rebuked Peter, saying, get thee behind me, Satan: for thou savourest not the things that be of God, but the things that be of men.

And when he had called the people unto him with his disciples also, he said unto them, whosoever will come after me, let him deny himself, and take up his cross, and follow me.

For whosoever will save his life shall lose it; but whosoever shall lose his life for my sake and the gospel's, the same shall save it.

For what shall it profit a man, if he shall gain the whole world, and lose his own soul?

Or what shall a man give in exchange for his soul?

Whosoever therefore shall be ashamed of me and of my words in this adulterous and sinful generation; of him also shall the Son of man be ashamed, when he cometh in the glory of his Father with the holy angels.

And he said unto them, Verily I say unto you, that there be some of them that stand here, which shall not taste of death, till they have seen the kingdom of God come with power.
(Mark 8: 31 – 38; Mark 9: 1 KJV)

The Transfiguration

And after six days Jesus taketh Peter, James, and John his brother, and bringeth them up into a high mountain apart,

And was transfigured before them: and his face did shine as the sun, and his raiment was white as the light.

And, behold, there appeared unto them Moses and Elias talking with him.

Then answered Peter, and said unto Jesus, Lord, it is good for us to be here: if thou wilt, let us make here three tabernacles; one for thee, and one for Moses, and one for Elias.

While he yet spoke, behold, a bright cloud overshadowed them: and behold a voice out of the cloud, which said, this is my beloved Son, in whom I am well pleased; hear ye him.

And when the disciples heard it, they fell on their face, and were sore afraid.

And Jesus came and touched them, and said, Arise, and be not afraid.

And when they had lifted up their eyes, they saw no man, save Jesus only.

And as they came down from the mountain, Jesus charged them, saying, Tell the vision to no man, until the Son of man be risen again from the dead.
(Matthew 17: 1 – 9 KJV)

The transfiguration of Jesus was a unique display of His divine character and a glimpse of the glory he had before he came to earth in

human form. It was a visible sign in the presence of reliable witnesses of the reality of the power of God and the glory, which is Jesus.

Why Elijah has to Come First?

And his disciples asked him, saying, why then say the scribes that Elias must first come?

And Jesus answered and said unto them, Elias truly shall first come, and restore all things.

But I say unto you, That Elias is come already, and they knew him not, but have done unto him whatsoever they listed. Likewise, shall also the Son of man suffer of them.

Then the disciples understood that he spoke unto them of John the Baptist.
(Matthew 17: 10 – 13 KJV)

Jesus Heals an Epileptic Boy (Miracle 26)

And when they were come to the multitude, there came to him a certain man, kneeling down to him, and saying,

Lord, have mercy on my son: for he is lunatick, and sore vexed: for ofttimes he falleth into the fire, and oft into the water.

And I brought him to thy disciples, and they could not cure him.

Then Jesus answered and said, O faithless and perverse generation, how long shall I be with you? how long shall I suffer you? bring him hither to me.

And Jesus rebuked the devil; and he departed out of him: and the child was cured from that very hour.

Then came the disciples to Jesus apart, and said, why could not we cast him out?

And Jesus said unto them, Because of your unbelief: for verily I say unto you, If ye have faith as a grain of mustard seed, ye shall say unto this mountain, Remove hence to yonder place; and it shall remove; and nothing shall be impossible unto you.
(Matthew 17: 14 – 20 KJV)

Focus Questions

1	What did Jesus say that his disciples must do if they wanted to be his followers?	4	Whom did Jesus refer to when he said Elijah has already come?
2	Who appeared to Jesus during the time when he was transfigured?	5	Why couldn't the disciples drive out the demons?
3	Which disciples were with him at the time of transfiguration?	6	What is the significance of the transfiguration of Jesus?

Note:

Jesus spoke about achieving a lot with even a tiny amount of faith, and on the surface of it he appears to be referring to faith in God; if we subscribe to the basic belief that 'God is everywhere', then faith may take on a broader context in our lives – faith in our own abilities, faith in our families/friends, faith in nature, faith in humankind ...

Reflection

If we experience the love and forgiveness of God in a personal way, we can understand how our life can be changed dramatically by one touch from the Lord.

Chapter 17
Jesus Teaches His Disciples

Jesus trains his disciples to preach the good news.

Learning Outcome

- know who can become the greatest in the Kingdom of heaven
- know what Jesus taught about forgiving

Jesus Speaks of His Death for the Second Time.

And while they abode in Galilee, Jesus said unto them, The Son of man shall be betrayed into the hands of men:

And they shall kill him, and the third day he shall be raised again. And they were exceeding sorry.
(Matthew 17: 22 – 23 KJV)

Who is the Greatest in the Kingdom of Heaven?

At the same time came the disciples unto Jesus, saying, who is the greatest in the kingdom of heaven?

And Jesus called a little child unto him, and set him in the midst of them,

And said, Verily I say unto you, except ye be converted, and become as little children, ye shall not enter into the kingdom of heaven.

Whosoever therefore shall humble himself as this little child, the same is greatest in the kingdom of heaven.

And whoso shall receive one such little child in my name receiveth me.

But whoso shall offend one of these little ones which believe in me, it were better for him that a millstone were hanged about his neck, and that he were drowned in the depth of the sea.
(Matthew 18: 1-6 KJV)

Whoever is Not Against Us is For Us.

And John answered him, saying, Master, we saw one casting out devils in thy name, and he followeth not us: and we forbad him, because he followeth not us.

But Jesus said, forbid him not: for there is no man which a miracle in my name shall do, that can lightly speak evil of me.

For he that is not against us is on our part.

For whosoever shall give you a cup of water to drink in my name, because ye belong to Christ, verily I say unto you, he shall not lose his reward.
(Mark 9: 38-41 KJV)

Jesus Pays Temple Tax (Miracle 27)

And when they were come to Capernaum, they that received tribute money came to Peter, and said, Doth not your master pay tribute?

He saith, Yes. And when he was come into the house, Jesus prevented him, saying, what thinkest thou, Simon? of whom do the kings of the earth take custom or tribute? of their own children, or of strangers?

Peter saith unto him, Of strangers. Jesus saith unto him, then are the children free.

Notwithstanding, lest we should offend them, go thou to the sea, and cast an hook, and take up the fish that first cometh up; and when thou hast opened his mouth, thou shalt find a piece of money: that take, and give unto them for me and thee.
(Matthew 17: 24 – 27 KJV)

How Many Times to Forgive?

Moreover, if thy brother shall trespass against thee, go and tell him his fault between thee and him alone: if he shall hear thee, thou hast gained thy brother.

But if he will not hear thee, then take with thee one or two more, that in the mouth of two or three witnesses every word may be established.

And if he shall neglect to hear them, tell it unto the church: but if he neglect to hear the church, let him be unto thee as a heathen man and a publican.
(Matthew 18: 15 – 17 KJV)

Then Peter asked Jesus: "Lord, if my brother keeps on sinning against me, how many times I have to forgive him? Seven Times?

Jesus answered: "No, not seven times, but seventy times seven."
(Matthew 18: 21- 22 KJV)

The Unforgiving Servant (Parable 12)

The kingdom of heaven likened unto a certain king, which would take account of his servants.

And when he had begun to reckon, one was brought unto him, which owed him ten thousand talents.

But forasmuch as he had not to pay, his lord commanded him to be sold, and his wife, and children, and all that he had, and payment to be made.

The servant therefore fell down, and worshipped him, saying, Lord, have patience with me, and I will pay thee all.

Then the lord of that servant was moved with compassion, and loosed him, and forgave him the debt.

But the same servant went out, and found one of his fellow servants, which owed him an hundred pence: and he laid hands on him, and took him by the throat, saying, Pay me that thou owest.

And his fellow servant fell down at his feet, and besought him, saying, have patience with me, and I will pay thee all.

And he would not: but went and cast him into prison, till he should pay the debt.

So when his fellow servants saw what was done, they were very sorry, and came and told unto their lord all that was done.

Then his lord, after that he had called him, said unto him, O thou wicked servant, I forgave thee all that debt, because thou desiredst me:

Shouldest not thou also have had compassion on thy fellow servant, even as I had pity on thee?

And his lord was wroth, and delivered him to the tormentors, till he should pay all that was due unto him.

So likewise, shall my heavenly Father do also unto you, if ye from your hearts forgive not everyone his brother their trespasses.
(Matthew 18: 23- 35 KJV)

The wicked servant in the parable, although begging forgiveness from God, does not apply his faith and is ultimately not saved. He considered his debt and the master's forgiveness to be trivial.

Jesus Scolds the Unbelieving Towns

Then began him to upbraid the cities wherein most of his mighty works were done, because they repented not:

Woe unto thee, Chorazin! woe unto thee, Bethsaida! for if the mighty works, which were done in you, had been done in Tyre and Sidon, they would have repented long ago in sackcloth and ashes .But I say unto you, It shall be more tolerable for Tyre and Sidon at the day of judgment, than for you.

And thou, Capernaum, which art exalted unto heaven, shalt be brought down to hell: for if the mighty works, which have been done in thee, had been done in Sodom, it would have remained until this day.

But I say unto you, that it shall be more tolerable for the land of Sodom in the day of judgment, than for thee.

At that time Jesus answered and said, I thank thee, O Father, Lord of heaven and earth, because thou hast hid these things from the wise and prudent, and hast revealed them unto babes.

Even so, Father: for so it seemed good in thy sight.

All things are delivered unto me of my Father: and no man knoweth the Son, but the Father; neither knoweth any man the Father, save the Son, and he to whomsoever the Son will reveal him.
(Matthew 11: 20- 27 KJV)

Focus Questions

1	How did Jesus pay Temple tax?	3	What lesson is to be learned from the parable of the unforgiving servant?
2	How many times must one forgive his brother according to Jesus?	4	What did Jesus expect people to do after witnessing his miracles?

Note:

Mercy and forgiveness seem to be lessons that we find difficult to learn. Who is honestly able to say that he/she is likely to be able to forgive someone twice, let alone seventy times seven? Even when faced with the task of forgiving people close to us, we seem to have an innate tendency to mistrust and question motives, rather than first look for the good that can be found in everyone. The message Jesus is giving us is very fair – we cannot expect to be forgiven by God if we cannot forgive the people around us.

Reflection

People are different because God created them to be different. When we come across argumentative and hostile people, people who are cold and indifferent, or those who are demanding, we may start loving them instead of dreading them, if we could only find the goodness in such difficult people.

Chapter 18
More Preaching and a Miracle

Jesus continues preaching in parables and performs a miracle.

Learning Outcome

- know Jesus as the Good Shepherd
- know what one must do to receive eternal life

The Return of The Seventy

And the seventy returned again with joy, saying, Lord, even the devils are subject unto us through thy name.

And he said unto them, I beheld Satan as lightning fall from heaven.

Behold, I give unto you power to tread on serpents and scorpions, and over all the power of the enemy: and nothing shall by any means hurt you.

Notwithstanding in this rejoice not, that the spirits are subject unto you; but rather rejoice, because your names are written in heaven.
(Luke 10: 17 – 20 KJV)

The Woman Caught in Adultery

And likewise, in the morning he came again into the temple, and all the people came unto him; and he sat down and taught them.

And the scribes and Pharisees brought unto him a woman taken in adultery; and when they had set her in the midst,

They say unto him, Master, this woman was taken in adultery, in the very act.

Now Moses in the law commanded us, that such should be stoned: but what sayest thou?

This they said, tempting him, that they might have to accuse him. But Jesus stooped down, and with his finger wrote on the ground, as though he heard them not.

So when they continued asking him, he lifted up himself, and said unto them, He that is without sin among you, let him first cast a stone at her.

And again, he stooped down, and wrote on the ground.

And they which heard it, being convicted by their own conscience, went out one by one, beginning at the eldest, even unto the last: and Jesus was left alone, and the woman standing in the midst.

When Jesus had lifted up himself, and saw none but the woman, he said unto her, Woman, where are those thine accusers? hath no man condemned thee?

She said, No man, Lord. And Jesus said unto her, neither do I condemn thee: go, and sin no more.
(John 8: 2 – 11 KJV)

Jesus Heals a man Born Blind (Miracle 28)

And as Jesus passed by, he saw a man which was blind from his birth.

And his disciples asked him, saying, Master, who did sin, this man, or his parents, that he was born blind?

Jesus answered, neither hath this man sinned, nor his parents: but that the works of God should be made manifest in him.

When he had thus spoken, he spat on the ground, and made clay of the spittle, and he anointed the eyes of the blind man with the clay,

And said unto him, Go, wash in the pool of Siloam, (which is by interpretation, Sent.) He went his way therefore, and washed, and came seeing.
(John 9: 1 – 3, 6 – 7 KJV)

Therefore, said people unto him, how were thine eyes opened? He answered and said, A man that is called Jesus made clay, and anointed mine eyes, and said unto me, go to the pool of Siloam, and wash: and I went and washed, and I received sight.
(John 9: 10 – 11 KJV)

Therefore, said some of the Pharisees, this man is not of God, because he keepeth not the sabbath day. Others said, how can a man that is a sinner do such miracles? And there was a division among them.

They say unto the blind man again, what sayest thou of him, that he hath opened thine eyes? He said, He is a prophet.

But the Jews did not believe concerning him, that he had been blind, and received his sight, until they called the parents of him that had received his sight.

And they asked them, saying, Is this your son, who ye say was born blind? how then doth he now see?

His parents answered them and said, we know that this is our son, and that he was born blind:

But by what means he now seeth, we know not; or who hath opened his eyes, we know not: he is of age; ask him: he shall speak for himself.
(John 9: 16 – 21 KJV)

Then again called they the man that was blind, and said unto him, Give God the praise: we know that this man is a sinner.

He answered and said, whether he be a sinner or no, I know not: one thing I know, that, whereas I was blind, now I see.

Then said they to him again, what did he to thee? how opened he thine eyes?

He answered them, I have told you already, and ye did not hear: wherefore would ye hear it again? will ye also be his disciples?

Then they reviled him, and said, thou art his disciple; but we are Moses' disciples.

We know that God spoke unto Moses: as for this fellow, we know not from whence he is.

The man answered and said unto them, why herein is a marvelous thing, that ye know not from whence he is, and yet he hath opened mine eyes.

Now we know that God heareth not sinners: but if any man be a worshipper of God, and doeth his will, him he heareth.

Since the world began was it not heard that any man opened the eyes of one that was born blind.

If this man were not of God, he could do nothing.

They answered and said unto him, thou wast altogether born in sins, and dost thou teach us? And they cast him out.

Jesus heard that they had cast him out; and when he had found him, he said unto him, Dost thou believe on the Son of God?

He answered and said, who is he, Lord, that I might believe on him?

And Jesus said unto him, thou hast both seen him, and it is he that talketh with thee.

And he said, Lord, I believe. And he worshipped him.

And Jesus said, for judgment I am come into this world, that they which see not might see; and that they which see might be made blind.

And some of the Pharisees which were with him heard these words, and said unto him, are we blind also?

Jesus said unto them, if ye were blind, ye should have no sin: but now ye say, we see; therefore, your sin remaineth.
(John 9: 24 – 41 KJV)

The object of Jesus' mission was salvation to humanity; the moral effect of His life was judgment. He judged no one, and yet He judged everyone.

The blind man made to see illustrates that those who accept their lost condition can regain grace through God's power.

The light of the world (Jesus) convicts and converts; judges and saves. It dazzles all those who think that they see; it lightens all those who really felt their moral and spiritual blindness.

The self-righteous people like the Pharisees who refuse to accept Jesus continue in their blindness and sin.

The Parable of the Shepherd (Parable 13)

Verily, verily, I say unto you, He that entereth not by the door into the sheepfold, but climbeth up some other way, the same is a thief and a robber.

But he that entereth in by the door is the shepherd of the sheep.

To him the porter openeth; and the sheep hear his voice: and he calleth his own sheep by name, and leadeth them out.

And when he putteth forth his own sheep, he goeth before them, and the sheep follow him: for they know his voice.

And a stranger will they not follow but will flee from him: for they know not the voice of strangers.

This parable spoke Jesus unto them: but they understood not what things they were which he spoke unto them.

Then said Jesus unto them again, Verily, verily, I say unto you, I am the door of the sheep.

All that ever came before me are thieves and robbers: but the sheep did not hear them.

I am the door: by me if any man enter in, he shall be saved, and shall go in and out, and find pasture.

The thief cometh not, but for to steal, and to kill, and to destroy: I am come that they might have life, and that they might have it more abundantly.

I am the good shepherd: the good shepherd giveth his life for the sheep.

But he that is an hireling, and not the shepherd, whose own the sheep are not, seeth the wolf coming, and leaveth the sheep, and fleeth: and the wolf catcheth them, and scattereth the sheep.
(John 10: 1 – 12 KJV)

And other sheep I have, which are not of this fold: them also I must bring, and they shall hear my voice; and there shall be one-fold, and one shepherd.
(John 10: 16 KJV)

There will be many who will try to influence people's lives, but they will not have their welfare in mind. Jesus is the one who enters by the door and is the Good Shepherd. He makes sure that his sheep are well-fed and protected from danger. He will nurse his sheep when they are sick, calm them when they are agitated and give them peace. When sheep that should belong to his flock are missing, he will search for them and when they hear his voice, they will join him.

What Must We Do to Enter Eternal Life?

And, behold, one came and said unto him, Good Master, what good thing shall I do, that I may have eternal life?

And he said unto him, why callest thou me good? there is none good but one, that is, God: but if thou wilt enter into life, keep the commandments.

He saith unto him, Which? Jesus said, thou shalt do no murder, thou shalt not commit adultery, Thou shalt not steal, Thou shalt not bear false witness, Honor thy father and thy mother: and, Thou shalt love thy neighbor as thyself.

The young man saith unto him, all these things have I kept from my youth up: what lack I yet?

Jesus said unto him, if thou wilt be perfect, go and sell that thou hast, and give to the poor, and thou shalt have treasure in heaven: and come and follow me.

But when the young man heard that saying, he went away sorrowful: for he had great possessions.
(Matthew 19: 16 – 22 KJV)

Focus Questions

1	What lesson is to be learned from the story of 'woman caught in adultery'?	4	What did Jesus answer to the question 'Whose sin made him to be born blind'?
2	What must one do to enter eternal life?	5	What did Jesus tell the woman caught in adultery?
3	Why Jesus is called the Good Shepherd?	6	What did Jesus mean when he said, 'I came to this world so that the blind should see and those who see should become blind'?

Note:

We are at times like the Pharisees who seemed to miss the greatness of the miracle that gave the blind man sight and we're more concerned about trying to fit the event into their sphere of understanding. Does it really matter if we don't always understand why or how something good, or bad, happened? Is there a benefit in rationalizing and justifying events? It is like wondering why the designer of a rollercoaster put a loop in a particular spot, rather than just enjoying the ride.

Reflection

Jesus is the Good Shepherd. He will protect and lead us to live a peaceful, compassionate and generous life if we trust him, and acknowledge him and his teachings. Shouldn't we then leave our cares to him trusting in him completely?

Chapter 19
Jesus Explains

The relative difficulty for the rich to enter the kingdom of heaven and the greatest commandment are explained by Jesus.

Learning Outcome

- know what Jesus said about entering the Kingdom of heaven
- know the greatest commandment in the scriptures

Entering the Kingdom of Heaven

Then said Jesus unto his disciples, Verily I say unto you, that a rich man shall hardly enter into the kingdom of heaven.

And again, I say unto you, it is easier for a camel to go through the eye of a needle, than for a rich man to enter into the kingdom of God.

When his disciples heard it, they were exceedingly amazed, saying, "who then can be saved"?

But Jesus beheld them, and said unto them, with men this is impossible; but with God all things are possible.
(Matthew 19: 23-26 KJV)

Jesus wanted to teach His disciples about money and its effects upon the likelihood of entering heaven. He compares the likelihood of a rich man entering heaven with that of a camel passing through the eye of a needle.

A gate in Jerusalem was called the "needle's eye" and was low and narrow, requiring a man to dismount his camel and the camel to get on its knees to enter through the gate.

Jesus' intent is to emphasize that it is impossible for a rich man to enter heaven by his own strength. Money tends to influence most people to the point that those who are rich are particularly susceptible to apathy, indifference, or even animosity when it comes to Jesus. In this way it is impossible for a rich man to enter heaven. If he were saying anything less than "impossible", the disciples would not likely be astonished and wonder who could be saved. The response of the disciples adds further evidence that Jesus did intend to say exactly what is recorded. If it were not for the wonderful grace of God that woos us to Himself, no one would be saved. Therefore, Jesus' answer was to say, "With man this is impossible, but with God all things are possible."

Reward for Those Who Left Everything

Then answered Peter and said unto him, Behold, we have forsaken all, and followed thee; what shall we have therefore?

And Jesus said unto them, Verily I say unto you, that ye which have followed me, in the regeneration when the Son of man shall sit in the throne of his glory, ye also shall sit upon twelve thrones, judging the twelve tribes of Israel.

And everyone that hath forsaken houses, or brethren, or sisters, or father, or mother, or wife, or children, or lands, for my name's sake, shall receive an hundredfold, and shall inherit everlasting life.
(Matthew 19: 27- 2 9 KJV)

The Greatest Commandment

The parable of the Good Samaritan (Parable 14)

And, behold, a certain lawyer stood up, and tempted him, saying, Master, what shall I do to inherit eternal life?

He said unto him, what is written in the law? how readest thou?

And he answering said, thou shalt love the Lord thy God with all thy heart, and with all thy soul, and with all thy strength, and with all thy mind; and thy neighbor as thyself.

And he said unto him, thou hast answered right: this do, and thou shalt live.

But he, willing to justify himself, said unto Jesus, and who is my neighbor?

And Jesus answering said, A certain man went down from Jerusalem to Jericho, and fell among thieves, which stripped him of his raiment, and wounded him, and departed, leaving him half dead.

And by chance there came down a certain priest that way: and when he saw him, he passed by on the other side.

And likewise, a Levite, when he was at the place, came and looked on him, and passed by on the other side.

But a certain Samaritan, as he journeyed, came where he was: and when he saw him, he had compassion on him,

And went to him, and bound up his wounds, pouring in oil and wine, and set him on his own beast, and brought him to an inn, and took care of him.

And on the morrow when he departed, he took out two pence, and gave them to the host, and said unto him, take care of him; and whatsoever thou spendest more, when I come again, I will repay thee.

Which now of these three, thinkest thou, was neighbor unto him that fell among the thieves?

And he said, He that shewed mercy on him. Then said Jesus unto him, Go, and do thou likewise.
(Luke 10: 25-37 KJV)

The lessons to be learned from the parable of the Good Samaritan are:

1. We must set aside our prejudice and show love and compassion for others and especially for those who are in need.
2. Our neighbor is anyone and so we must love all of mankind.

The Question About the Messiah

While the Pharisees were gathered together, Jesus asked them,

Saying, what think ye of Christ? whose son is he? They say unto him, The son of David.

He saith unto them, how then doth David in spirit call him Lord, saying,

The Lord said unto my Lord, sit thou on my right hand, till I make thine enemies thy footstool?

If David then call him Lord, how is he his son?

And no man was able to answer him a word, neither durst any man from that day forth ask him any more questions.
(Matthew 22: 41-46 KJV)

Jesus Visits Martha and Mary

Now it came to pass, as they went, that he entered into a certain village: and a certain woman named Martha received him into her house.

And she had a sister called Mary, which also sat at Jesus' feet, and heard his word.

But Martha was cumbered about much serving, and came to him, and said, Lord, dost thou not care that my sister hath left me to serve alone? bid her therefore that she help me.

And Jesus answered and said unto her, Martha, Martha, thou art careful and troubled about many things:

But one thing is needful: and Mary hath chosen that good part, which shall not be taken away from her.
(Luke 10: 38-42 KJV)

The Demand for A Miracle

Then certain of the scribes and of the Pharisees answered, saying, Master, we would see a sign from thee.

But he answered and said unto them, an evil and adulterous generation seeketh after a sign; and there shall no sign be given to it, but the sign of the prophet Jonas:

For as Jonas was three days and three nights in the whale's belly; so, shall the Son of man be three days and three nights in the heart of the earth.

The men of Nineveh shall rise in judgment with this generation and shall condemn it: because they repented at the preaching of Jonas; and, behold, a greater than Jonas is here.

The queen of the south shall rise in the judgment with this generation and shall condemn it: for she came from the uttermost parts of the earth to hear the wisdom of Solomon; and, behold, a greater than Solomon is here. (Matthew 12: 38-42 KJV)

Same State as When an Evil Spirit Returns

When the unclean spirit is gone out of a man, he walketh through dry places, seeking rest; and finding none, he saith, I will return unto my house whence I came out.

And when he cometh, he findeth it swept and garnished.

Then goeth he, and taketh to him seven other spirits more wicked than himself; and they enter in, and dwell there: and the last state of that man is worse than the first.

And it came to pass, as he spoke these things, a certain woman of the company lifted up her voice, and said unto him, blessed is the womb that bare thee, and the paps which thou hast sucked.

But he said, yea rather, blessed are they that hear the word of God, and keep it.
(Luke 11: 24-28 KJV)

Focus Questions

1	Why do you think Jesus said that it is easier for a camel to go through the eye of the Needle than a rich man to enter heaven?	3	What answer did Jesus give when the teachers of the Law said to him "Teacher, we want to see you perform a miracle."?
2	What answer did Jesus give when Peter asked '"we have left everything and followed you. What will we have"?	4	How did Jesus answer the question: "Who is my neighbor"?

Note:

The message of the parable about the neighbor seems to be missed by a lot of people in today's society. Even popular sayings are incongruous with the principle Jesus was preaching – for example 'charity begins at home' tells us to look after our own family or friends first; but it is much more difficult to be generous to someone we don't know, like the Samaritan. Our true character shows when we reach out to people from whom we cannot gain anything.

Reflection

How can we love our enemies? How can we love those who have opposed us or hurt us? How are we supposed to love people with conflicting views, competing religious beliefs, or radically different ethnic backgrounds? The answer is 'through Jesus'. By His grace, he has made us capable of showering everyone with his forgiveness, kindness and love – even those who happen to dislike us and/or what we stand for. Every time you treat someone the way you want to be treated, regardless of how you feel, God's grace flows through you.

Chapter 20
Jesus Rebukes

Jesus gets harsh with the teachers of the Law.

Learning Outcome

- know the importance of piling up riches in God's sight
- know the importance of being fruitful in life
- know that honesty is better than hypocrisy

The Rich Fool (Parable 15)

And one of the company said unto him, Master, speak to my brother, that he divides the inheritance with me.

And he said unto him, Man, who made me a judge or a divider over you?

And he said unto them, take heed, and beware of covetousness: for a man's life consisteth not in the abundance of the things which he possesseth.

And he spoke a parable unto them, saying, the ground of a certain rich man brought forth plentifully:

And he thought within himself, saying, what shall I do, because I have no room where to bestow my fruits?

And he said, this will I do: I will pull down my barns and build greater; and there will I bestow all my fruits and my goods.

And I will say to my soul, Soul, thou hast much goods laid up for many years; take thine ease, eat, drink, and be merry.

But God said unto him, thou fool, this night thy soul shall be required of thee: then whose shall those things be, which thou hast provided?

So is he that layeth up treasure for himself and is not rich toward God. (Luke 12: 13-21 KJV)

This parable is a stern warning against greed. It emphasizes the folly of covetousness in any form and the error of thinking that a man's life is measured by the abundance of things he possessed.

The Unfruitful Fig Tree (Parable 16)

He spoke also this parable; A certain man had a fig tree planted in his vineyard; and he came and sought fruit thereon and found none.

Then said he unto the dresser of his vineyard, Behold, these three years I come seeking fruit on this fig tree, and find none: cut it down; why cumbereth it the ground?

And he answering said unto him, Lord, let it alone this year also, till I shall dig about it, and dung it:

And if it bears fruit, well: and if not, then after that thou shalt cut it down (Luke 13: 6-9 KJV)

The parable warns that Judgment is coming. The unproductive and the unfruitful will be cut down. The vineyard owner (God the Father) is severe with those who are disobedient and fail to bear fruit. The gardener (God the Son) gives opportunity and encouragement for the unfruitful and disobedient to repent. The gardener's plea on behalf of the condemned fig tree represents the intercession of Jesus for us.

In this parable, the fruitless fig tree represents sinners, Vineyard the whole earth, fig tree the Jewish people and the gardener is Jesus.

Jesus Heals a Crippled Woman (Miracle 29)

And he was teaching in one of the synagogues on the sabbath.

And, behold, there was a woman which had a spirit of infirmity eighteen years, and was bowed together, and could in no wise lift up herself.

And when Jesus saw her, he called her to him, and said unto her, Woman, thou art loosed from thine infirmity.

And he laid his hands on her: and immediately she was made straight, and glorified God.

And the ruler of the synagogue answered with indignation, because that Jesus had healed on the sabbath day, and said unto the people, there are six days in which men ought to work: in them therefore come and be healed, and not on the sabbath day.

The Lord then answered him, and said, thou hypocrite, doth not each one of you on the sabbath loose his ox or his ass from the stall, and lead him away to watering?

And ought not this woman, being a daughter of Abraham, whom Satan hath bound, lo, these eighteen years, be loosed from this bond on the sabbath day?

And when he had said these things, all his adversaries were ashamed: and all the people rejoiced for all the glorious things that were done by him. (Luke 13: 10-17 KJV)

Jesus Condemns the Hypocrisy

Then spoke Jesus to the multitude, and to his disciples, saying the scribes and the Pharisees sit in Moses' seat:

All therefore whatsoever they bid you observe, that observe and do; but do not ye after their works: for they say, and do not.

For they bind heavy burdens and grievous to be borne and lay them on men's shoulders; but they themselves will not move them with one of their fingers.

But all their works they do for to be seen of men: they make broad their phylacteries, and enlarge the borders of their garments,

And love the uppermost rooms at feasts, and the chief seats in the synagogues,

And greetings in the markets, and to be called of men, Rabbi, Rabbi.

But be not ye called Rabbi: for one is your Master, even Christ; and all ye are brethren.

And call no man your father upon the earth: for one is your Father, which is in heaven.

Neither be ye called masters: for one is your Master, even Christ. (Matthew 23: 1-10 KJV)

Jesus Curses the Teachers and the Pharisees

But woe unto you, scribes and Pharisees, hypocrites! for ye shut up the kingdom of heaven against men: for ye neither go in yourselves, neither suffer ye them that are entering to go in.

Woe unto you, scribes and Pharisees, hypocrites! for ye devour widows' houses, and for a pretence make long prayer: therefore, ye shall receive the greater damnation.

Woe unto you, scribes and Pharisees, hypocrites! for ye compass sea and land to make one proselyte, and when he is made, ye make him twofold more the child of hell than yourselves.

Woe unto you, ye blind guides, which say, whosoever shall swear by the temple, it is nothing; but whosoever shall swear by the gold of the temple, he is a debtor!

Ye fools and blind: for whether is greater, the gold, or the temple that sanctifieth the gold?

And, whosoever shall swear by the altar, it is nothing; but whosoever sweareth by the gift that is upon it, he is guilty.

Ye fools and blind: for whether is greater, the gift, or the altar that sanctifieth the gift?

Whoso therefore shall swear by the altar, sweareth by it, and by all things thereon.

And whoso shall swear by the temple, sweareth by it, and by him that dwelleth therein.

And he that shall swear by heaven, sweareth by the throne of God, and by him that sitteth thereon.

Woe unto you, scribes and Pharisees, hypocrites! for ye pay tithe of mint and anise and cummin, and have omitted the weightier matters of the law, judgment, mercy, and faith: these ought ye to have done, and not to leave the other undone.

Ye blind guides, which strain at a gnat, and swallow a camel.

Woe unto you, scribes and Pharisees, hypocrites! for ye make clean the outside of the cup and of the platter, but within they are full of extortion and excess.

Thou blind Pharisee, cleanse first that which is within the cup and platter, that the outside of them may be clean also.

Woe unto you, scribes and Pharisees, hypocrites! for ye are like unto whited sepulchres, which indeed appear beautiful outward, but are within full of dead men's bones, and of all uncleanness.

Even so ye also outwardly appear righteous unto men, but within ye are full of hypocrisy and iniquity.

Woe unto you, scribes and Pharisees, hypocrites! because ye build the tombs of the prophets, and garnish the sepulchres of the righteous,

And say, If we had been in the days of our fathers, we would not have been partakers with them in the blood of the prophets.

Wherefore ye be witnesses unto yourselves, that ye are the children of them which killed the prophets.

Fill ye up then the measure of your fathers.

Ye serpents, ye generation of vipers, how can ye escape the damnation of hell?

Wherefore, behold, I send unto you prophets, and wise men, and scribes: and some of them ye shall kill and crucify; and some of them shall ye scourge in your synagogues, and persecute them from city to city:

That upon you may come all the righteous blood shed upon the earth, from the blood of righteous Abel unto the blood of Zacharias son of Barachias, whom ye slew between the temple and the altar.

Verily I say unto you, all these things shall come upon this generation.

(Matthew 23: 13-36 KJV)

Jesus Reprimands Jerusalem

O Jerusalem, Jerusalem, thou that killest the prophets, and stonest them which are sent unto thee, how often would I have gathered thy children together, even as a hen gathereth her chickens under her wings, and ye would not!

Behold, your house is left unto you desolate.

For I say unto you, Ye shall not see me henceforth, till ye shall say, blessed is he that cometh in the name of the Lord.
(Matthew 23: 37-39 KJV)

Focus Questions

1	What would happen to those who pile up worldly riches but not spiritual riches in God's sight?	3	Why was Jesus mad at the Pharisees and the teachers of the Law?
2	What lesson can be learned from the parable of the unfruitful fig tree?	4	What answer did Jesus give when he was questioned about healing the crippled woman on a Sabbath day?

Note:

Jesus' intolerance of hypocrites could not be more appropriate; how commonly do we see ourselves guilty of hypocrisy? Is it better to be true to ourselves even when Society's norm disagrees, or should we conform despite our instincts? As long as we are sure that our intentions are pure, honesty surely must be better than hypocrisy, no matter what the consequences to ourselves.

Reflection

Hypocrisy is denying or overlooking truth (the truth about ourselves, about the world around us) in order to derive some benefit or satisfaction, or to avoid disbenefit or dissatisfaction. If we are to avoid the sin, we commit through hypocrisy we must have the humility to submit to God and seek help with our struggles.

Chapter 21
Jesus Tells More Parables

There is great joy in heaven when a sinner repents.

Learning Outcome

- know what Jesus is trying to teach us through the parables in this chapter

The Parable of the Lost Sheep (Parable 17)

How think ye? if a man have an hundred sheep, and one of them be gone astray, doth he not leave the ninety and nine, and goeth into the mountains, and seeketh that which is gone astray?

And if so be that he find it, verily I say unto you, he rejoiceth more of that sheep, than of the ninety and nine which went not astray.

Even so it is not the will of your Father which is in heaven, that one of these little ones should perish.
(Matthew 18: 12-14 KJV)

The Parable of the Lost Coin (Parable 18)

What woman having ten pieces of silver, if she loses one piece, doth not light a candle, and sweep the house, and seek diligently till she find it?

And when she hath found it, she calleth her friends and her neighbors together, saying, rejoice with me; for I have found the piece which I had lost.

Likewise, I say unto you, there is joy in the presence of the angels of God over one sinner that repenteth.
(Luke 15: 8-10 KJV)

The Parable of the Lost Son (Parable 19)

And he said, A certain man had two sons:

And the younger of them said to his father, Father, give me the portion of goods that falleth to me. And he divided unto them his living.

And not many days after the younger son gathered all together, and took his journey into a far country, and there wasted his substance with riotous living.

And when he had spent all, there arose a mighty famine in that land; and he began to be in want.

And he went and joined himself to a citizen of that country; and he sent him into his fields to feed swine.

And he would fain have filled his belly with the husks that the swine did eat: and no man gave unto him.

And when he came to himself, he said, how many hired servants of my father have bread enough and to spare, and I perish with hunger!

I will arise and go to my father, and will say unto him, Father, I have sinned against heaven, and before thee,

And am no more worthy to be called thy son: make me as one of thy hired servants.

And he arose and came to his father. But when he was yet a great way off, his father saw him, and had compassion, and ran, and fell on his neck, and kissed him.

And the son said unto him, Father, I have sinned against heaven, and in thy sight, and am no more worthy to be called thy son.

But the father said to his servants, bring forth the best robe, and put it on him; and put a ring on his hand, and shoes on his feet:

And bring hither the fatted calf, and kill it; and let us eat, and be merry:

For this my son was dead, and is alive again; he was lost, and is found. And they began to be merry.

Now his elder son was in the field: and as he came and drew nigh to the house, he heard music and dancing.

And he called one of the servants and asked what these things meant.

And he said unto him, thy brother is come; and thy father hath killed the fatted calf, because he hath received him safe and sound.

And he was angry, and would not go in: therefore, came his father out, and intreated him.

And he answering said to his father, Lo, these many years do I serve thee, neither transgressed I at any time thy commandment: and yet thou never gavest me a kid, that I might make merry with my friends:

But as soon as this thy son was come, which hath devoured thy living with harlots, thou hast killed for him the fatted calf.

And he said unto him, Son, thou art ever with me, and all that I have is thine.

It was meet that we should make merry and be glad: for this thy brother was dead, and is alive again; and was lost, and is found.
(Luke 15: 11-32 KJV)

The parables of the lost sheep and the lost coin, both illustrate the point that God rejoices about each sinner who repents. The long parable of the lost son continues the theme of rejoicing and adds to it. In the first two parables, the lost were found by searching. But the younger son was found by waiting for the son to realize his folly and to return to his father. The spiritually lost were already coming to Jesus; he didn't need to seek them out. They had been spiritually dead and were now showing interest. They wanted to be taught by Jesus. Jesus received them and ate with them. His reception would have encouraged them to keep the laws they already knew and to continue to listen to him for more instruction in God's way.

The parable of the lost son shows that sinners can confess and return to God. Since God is gracious, sinners can return to him with confidence that he will warmly welcome and accept them. Most importantly, the parable shows that God's people should rejoice at (a) the willingness of sinners to turn to God and (b) the willingness of God to receive them. This is the lesson of the second half of the parable, illustrated by the father's correction of his older son. This theme most directly addresses the setting of the parable, the Pharisees' criticism of Jesus' reception of sinners. The parables of the lost sheep and lost coin and the first half of the parable of the lost son are preparatory to this main point.

The Shrewd Steward (Parable 20)

And he said also unto his disciples, there was a certain rich man, which had a steward; and the same was accused unto him that he had wasted his goods.

And he called him, and said unto him, how is it that I hear this of thee? give an account of thy stewardship; for thou mayest be no longer steward.

Then the steward said within himself, what shall I do? for my lord taketh away from me the stewardship: I cannot dig; to beg I am ashamed.

I am resolved what to do, that, when I am put out of the stewardship, they may receive me into their houses.

So, he called every one of his Lord's debtors unto him, and said unto the first, How much owest thou unto my lord?

And he said, A hundred measures of oil. And he said unto him, take thy bill, and sit down quickly, and write fifty.

Then said he to another, And how much owest thou? And he said, A hundred measures of wheat. And he said unto him, take thy bill, and write fourscore.

And the lord commended the unjust steward, because he had done wisely: for the children of this world are in their generation wiser than the children of light.

And I say unto you, make to yourselves friends of the mammon of unrighteousness; that, when ye fail, they may receive you into everlasting habitations.

He that is faithful in that which is least is faithful also in much: and he that is unjust in the least is unjust also in much.

If therefore ye have not been faithful in the unrighteous mammon, who will commit to your trust the true riches?

And if ye have not been faithful in that which is another man's, who shall give you that which is your own?

And the Pharisees also, who were covetous, heard all these things: and they derided him.

And he said unto them, Ye are they which justify yourselves before men; but God knoweth your hearts: for that which is highly esteemed among men is abomination in the sight of God.
(Luke 16: 1-12, 14-15 KJV)

This story from Jesus was meant to provide a sort of "management model" for the disciples'—for their own roles and relationships in the world. Jesus, instead of hoisting upon them a lifestyle of scarcity, or burdening them with an abstract ideal of poverty, or advising them on how to keep themselves pure from the contaminations of unjust wealth, challenged them instead through this parable of the Shrewd Steward, to manage wealth in the direction of integrity, and to manage wealth in the direction of honesty and to manage wealth in the direction of justice; for in and through such a process, the disciples would be creating new communities and new relationships that would allow their mission to go forward and that would support the enjoyment, and the enrichment, of abundant life for all!

The Rich man and Lazarus (Parable 21)

There was a certain rich man, which was clothed in purple and fine linen, and fared sumptuously every day:

And there was a certain beggar named Lazarus, which was laid at his gate, full of sores,

And desiring to be fed with the crumbs which fell from the rich man's table: moreover, the dogs came and licked his sores.

And it came to pass, that the beggar died, and was carried by the angels into Abraham's bosom: the rich man also died, and was buried;

And in hell he lift up his eyes, being in torments, and seeth Abraham afar off, and Lazarus in his bosom.

And he cried and said, Father Abraham, have mercy on me, and send Lazarus, that he may dip the tip of his finger in water, and cool my tongue; for I am tormented in this flame.

But Abraham said, Son, remember that thou in thy lifetime receivedst thy good things, and likewise Lazarus evil things: but now he is comforted, and thou art tormented.

And beside all this, between us and you there is a great gulf fixed: so that they which would pass from hence to you cannot; neither can they pass to us, that would come from thence.

Then he said, I pray thee therefore, father, that thou wouldest send him to my father's house:

For I have five brethren; that he may testify unto them, lest they also come into this place of torment.

Abraham saith unto him, they have Moses and the prophets; let them hear them.

And he said, Nay, father Abraham: but if one went unto them from the dead, they will repent.

And he said unto him, If they hear not Moses and the prophets, neither will they be persuaded, though one rose from the dead.
(Luke 16: 19-31 KJV)

The clothing and the luxurious living of the rich man identifies him symbolically with the people of Israel, who God chose to be a special people. They were called to be witnesses to the nations surrounding them, confirming the blessings available to those who would obey God and keep His laws.

In contrast to the rich man is Lazarus. The first thing to note is that he is depicted as a beggar. This is an apt description of the Gentiles.

Additionally, we are told that dogs came and consoled Lazarus in his misery, licking his sores. The Jews considered the surrounding Gentiles to be unclean "dogs."

Jesus used this story, which fit the common misconception about life after death in his day, to show the fate that awaited the Jewish nation because of the unbelief which led them to reject him as the Messiah.

Jesus uses the last two verses of this parable as an amazing prophecy of his pending resurrection from the dead. The rich man says that although his brothers may not accept the scriptural evidence for the identity of the Messiah, they will accept the evidence of one who is raised from the dead.

But Abraham answers and plainly tells him that anyone who rejects God's Word about the Messiah will also refuse to acknowledge the evidence of a miraculous resurrection. This last verse is a sad prophecy about the Jews and about all the Israelites who have not, despite God's resurrection of His son from the power of the grave, recognized Jesus as the Messiah.

The Unprofitable Servants (Parable 22)

Jesus continued:

But which of you, having a servant plowing or feeding cattle, will say unto him by and by, when he is come from the field, Go and sit down to meat?

And will not rather say unto him, make ready wherewith I may sup, and gird thyself, and serve me, till I have eaten and drunken; and afterward thou shalt eat and drink?

Doth he thank that servant because he did the things that were commanded him? I trow not.

So likewise, ye, when ye shall have done all those things which are commanded you, say, We are unprofitable servants: we have done that which was our duty to do.

(Luke 17: 7-10 KJV)

This parable reminds us of the need for obedience to God's commandments and that no matter how much we do for the Lord we are still "unprofitable servants". Therefore, whatever reward we receive will be one of grace and not merit; and what wonderful grace that will be, to hear the Lord say at the end of time: "Well done, good and faithful servant"

Ten Men Healed from Skin Disease (Miracle 30)

Now it happened as He went to Jerusalem that He passed through the midst of Samaria and Galilee. Then as He entered a certain village, there met Him ten men who were lepers, who stood afar off. And they lifted up their voices and said, "Jesus, Master, have mercy on us!"

So, when He saw them, He said to them, "Go, show yourselves to the priests." And so, it was that as they went, they were cleansed.

And one of them, when he saw that he was healed, returned, and with a loud voice glorified God,6 and fell down on his face at His feet, giving Him thanks. And he was a Samaritan.

So, Jesus answered and said, "Were there not ten cleansed? But where are the nine? Were there not any found who returned to give glory to God except this foreigner?" And He said to him, "Arise, go your way. Your faith has made you well."
(Luke 17: 11-19 KJV)

Healing by Jesus was an important means of conveying his message, along with parables, sermons, and other means. It was possibly the primary reason that most people came to see him, either to be healed or drawn in awe by his reputation for healing.

The instruction to "Go and let the priests examine you" is to follow the original Mosaic Law. Giving praise to God, who has healed them, rather than spreading the word around to others, is the right thing to do; but only one in ten has done this. One must feel ashamed of the behavior as displayed by the other nine. The nine might have thought that they deserved cure because they were God's chosen people and of course they were very ungrateful.

Focus Questions

1	What message is Jesus trying to give through the parables of: (a) The lost sheep (b) The lost coin (c) The Lost son?	3	What does the parable of the unprofitable servant remind us?
2	What can we learn from the parable of the shrewd steward?	4	Why do you think that nine of the ten men cured of skin disease did not thank Jesus?

Note:

When reading the parables, one must remember the two levels of meaning they carry and not take the literal interpretation only.

The parable of the lost son clearly aims to show God's attitude towards sinners who return to God, however, many of us would identify with the other son who feels that his loyalty has been taken for granted. Surely the 'unprofitable servant' must feel similarly, and we may find it hard to acknowledge that God would want us to act like that towards anyone in our own lives.

The story about the rich man and Lazarus seems to suggest that the rich man will suffer in the life after death, with no obvious consideration of his actions in this life. Does this mean that having worldly wealth is disadvantageous, even if one leads a pure and well-intentioned life? This appears to be at odds with the parable of the shrewd steward.

The parable of the shrewd steward demonstrates the association between responsibility with worldly wealth and responsibility with spiritual wealth.

If taken literally, these conflicting themes could be confusing. Perhaps the conflict is a realistic reflection of the complexity of our lives, with no single message or theme being able to cater for every situation that we find confronting us. Adaptability and understanding of the underlying principles Jesus was teaching, rather than rigid adherence to specific rules, would be the key.

Reflection

Human struggle is part of God's plan. Obeying his commandments while enduring the struggle helps us become mature and complete as He wants us to be. When the struggle seems overwhelming, Jesus is with us, helping us and guiding us.

Chapter 22
The Kingdom, Power and Glory

Jesus teaches among other things about the nature of the Kingdom of heaven, and the method to pray.

Learning Outcome

- know the nature of the Kingdom of God
- know what Jesus said about praying
- know what Jesus said about unmarried men
- know what Jesus said about divorce

The Coming of the Kingdom

And he said unto the disciples, the days will come, when ye shall desire to see one of the days of the Son of man, and ye shall not see it.

And they shall say to you, see here; or, see there: go not after them, nor follow them.

For as the lightning, that lighteneth out of the one part under heaven, shineth unto the other part under heaven; so, shall also the Son of man be in his day.

But first must he suffer many things and be rejected of this generation.

And as it was in the days of Noe, so shall it be also in the days of the Son of man.

They did eat, they drank, they married wives, they were given in marriage, until the day that Noah entered into the ark, and the flood came, and destroyed them all.

Likewise, also as it was in the days of Lot; they did eat, they drank, they bought, they sold, they planted, they builded;

But the same day that Lot went out of Sodom it rained fire and brimstone from heaven and destroyed them all.

Even thus shall it be in the day when the Son of man is revealed.

In that day, he which shall be upon the housetop, and his stuff in the house, let him not come down to take it away: and he that is in the field, let him likewise not return back.

Remember Lot's wife.

Whosoever shall seek to save his life shall lose it; and whosoever shall lose his life shall preserve it.

I tell you, in that night there shall be two men in one bed; the one shall be taken, and the other shall be left.

Two women shall be grinding together; the one shall be taken, and the other left.

Two men shall be in the field; the one shall be taken, and the other left.

And they answered and said unto him, Where, Lord? And he said unto them, Wheresoever the body is, thither will the eagles be gathered together. (Luke 17: 22-37 KJV)

The dominant theme in the preaching of Jesus is the coming of the Kingdom of God. This term has both present and future associations. Jesus says that the Kingdom is present, and it is present in him.

Jesus also tells us three things about his coming in the future:

It is not going to be secret. It's going to be dramatic and obvious

It is going to be sudden, with no warning, no advance notice.

It is going to divide the closest of family ties, friendship ties and proximity ties.

The Corrupt Judge – The Persistent Widow (Parable 23)

And he spoke a parable unto them to this end, that men ought always to pray, and not to faint; Saying, there was in a city a judge, which feared not God, neither regarded man:

And there was a widow in that city; and she came unto him, saying, Avenge me of mine adversary.
And he would not for a while: but afterward he said within himself, Though I fear not God, nor regard man;
Yet because this widow troubleth me, I will avenge her, lest by her continual coming, she weary me.
And the Lord said, Hear what the unjust judge saith.

And shall not God avenge his own elect, which cry day and night unto him, though he bear long with them?

I tell you that he will avenge them speedily. Nevertheless, when the Son of man cometh, shall he find faith on the earth?
(Luke 18: 1-8 KJV)

The Pharisee and the Tax Collector (Parable 24)

And he spoke this parable unto certain which trusted in themselves that they were righteous, and despised others:

Two men went up into the temple to pray; the one a Pharisee, and the other a publican.

The Pharisee stood and prayed thus with himself, God, I thank thee, that I am not as other men are, extortioners, unjust, adulterers, or even as this publican.

I fast twice in the week, I give tithes of all that I possess.

And the publican, standing afar off, would not lift up so much as his eyes unto heaven, but smote upon his breast, saying, God be merciful to me a sinner.

I tell you, this man went down to his house justified rather than the other: for everyone that exalteth himself shall be abased; and he that humbleth himself shall be exalted.
(Luke 18: 9-14 KJV)

Ask, Seek, Knock

And he said unto them, which of you shall have a friend, and shall go unto him at midnight, and say unto him, Friend, lend me three loaves;

For a friend of mine in his journey is come to me, and I have nothing to set before him?

And he from within shall answer and say, Trouble me not: the door is now shut, and my children are with me in bed; I cannot rise and give thee.

I say unto you, though he will not rise and give him, because he is his friend, yet because of his importunity he will rise and give him as many as he needeth.

And so, I say to you: **Ask, and it shall be given you; seek, and ye shall find; knock, and it shall be opened unto you:**

For everyone that asketh receiveth; and he that seeketh findeth; and to him that knocketh it shall be opened.

Or what man is there of you, whom if his son ask bread, will he give him a stone?

Or if he ask a fish, will he give him a serpent?

If ye then, being evil, know how to give good gifts unto your children, how much more shall your Father which is in heaven give good things to them that ask him?
(Luke 11: 5-8; Matthew 7: 7-11)

The Power of Prayer

Again, I say unto you, that if two of you shall agree on earth as touching anything that they shall ask, it shall be done for them of my Father which is in heaven.

For where two or three are gathered together in my name, there am I in the midst of them.
(Matthew 18: 19-20 KJV)

Jesus Teaches About Divorce

The Pharisees also came unto him, tempting him, and saying unto him, is it lawful for a man to put away his wife for every cause?

And he answered and said unto them, have ye not read, that he which made them at the beginning made them male and female,

And said, for this cause shall a man leave father and mother, and shall cleave to his wife: and they twain shall be one flesh?

Wherefore they are no more twain, but one flesh. What therefore God hath joined together, let not man put asunder.

They say unto him, why did Moses then command to give a writing of divorcement, and to put her away?

He saith unto them, Moses because of the hardness of your hearts suffered you to put away your wives: but from the beginning it was not so.

And I say unto you, whosoever shall put away his wife, except it be for fornication, and shall marry another, committeth adultery: and whoso marrieth her which is put away doth commit adultery.
(Matthew 19: 3-9 KJV

And he saith unto them, whosoever shall put away his wife, and marry another, committeth adultery against her.

And if a woman shall put away her husband, and be married to another, she committeth adultery.
(Mark 10: 11-12 KJV)

Whosoever putteth away his wife, and marrieth another, committeth adultery: and whosoever marrieth her that is put away from her husband committeth adultery."
(Luke 16:18 KJV)

Unmarried men

His disciples say unto him, If the case of the man be so with his wife, it is not good to marry. But he said unto them, All men cannot receive this saying, save they to whom it is given.

For there are some eunuchs, which were so born from their mother's womb: and there are some eunuchs, which were made eunuchs of men: and there be eunuchs, which have made themselves eunuchs for the kingdom of heaven's sake. He that is able to receive it, let him receive it.
(Matthew 19: 10-12 KJV)

Jesus Blesses Little Children

And they brought unto him also infants, that he would touch them: but when his disciples saw it, they rebuked them.

But Jesus called them unto him, and said, suffer little children to come unto me and forbid them not: for of such is the kingdom of God.

Verily I say unto you, whosoever shall not receive the kingdom of God as a little child shall in no wise enter therein.
(Luke 18: 15-17)

Focus Questions

1	What did Jesus say about the coming of the Kingdom of God?	3	Summarize what Jesus said about praying.
2	How did Pharisee pray in the parable of the Pharisee and the Tax Collector?	4	What did Jesus say about divorce?

Reflection

There is a great difference between mere repetition of words in prayer and pleading earnestly and repeatedly. Jesus, in his parables, praises this and the firmness of purpose; He said, "He who asks receives, and he who seeks finds, and he who knocks will find it opened to him."

Chapter 23
Jesus's Power Over Death

After hearing about the extraordinary miracle Jesus performed, the Pharisees make plans to kill him.

Learning Outcome

Know the hidden meaning in the parable below

- know how Jesus proved his power over death
- know why the Jews wanted to kill Jesus
- know what Jesus said how he will be killed

The Workers in the Vineyard (Parable 25)

For the kingdom of heaven is like unto a man that is an householder, which went out early in the morning to hire laborers into his vineyard.

And when he had agreed with the laborers for a penny a day, he sent them into his vineyard.

And he went out about the third hour, and saw others standing idle in the marketplace,

And said unto them; Go ye also into the vineyard, and whatsoever is right I will give you. And they went their way.

Again, he went out about the sixth and ninth hour, and did likewise.

And about the eleventh hour he went out, and found others standing idle, and saith unto them, why stand ye here all the day idle?

They say unto him, because no man hath hired us. He saith unto them, go ye also into the vineyard; and whatsoever is right, that shall ye receive.

So, when even was come, the lord of the vineyard saith unto his steward, Call the laborer, and give them their hire, beginning from the last unto the first.

And when they came that were hired about the eleventh hour, they received every man a penny.

But when the first came, they supposed that they should have received more; and they likewise received every man a penny.

And when they had received it, they murmured against the good man of the house,

Saying, these last have wrought but one hour, and thou hast made them equal unto us, which have borne the burden and heat of the day.

But he answered one of them, and said, Friend, I do thee no wrong: didst not thou agree with me for a penny?

Take that thine is and go thy way: I will give unto this last, even as unto thee.

Is it not lawful for me to do what I will with mine own? Is thine eye evil, because I am good?

So the last shall be first, and the first last: for many be called, but few chosen.
(Matthew 20: 1-16 KJV)

Some people will believe in Jesus and follow him early in life, while others will believe and follow him later in life. But the reward will be

the same; to spend eternity with Jesus. It is not the length of time that we have believed in Jesus or the amount of work that we have done for him that makes us right with God.

Jesus Raises Lazarus (Miracle 31)

Now a certain man was sick, named Lazarus, of Bethany, the town of Mary and her sister Martha.
(It was that Mary which anointed the Lord with ointment, and wiped his feet with her hair, whose brother Lazarus was sick.)

Therefore, his sisters sent unto him, saying, Lord, behold, he whom thou lovest is sick.

When Jesus heard that, he said, this sickness is not unto death, but for the glory of God, that the Son of God might be glorified thereby.

Now Jesus loved Martha, and her sister, and Lazarus.

When he had heard therefore that he was sick, he abode two days still in the same place where he was.

Then after that saith he to his disciples, let us go into Judaea again.

His disciples say unto him, Master, the Jews of late sought to stone thee; and goest thou thither again?

Jesus answered, Are there not twelve hours in the day? If any man walk in the day, he stumbleth not, because he seeth the light of this world.

But if a man walk in the night, he stumbleth, because there is no light in him.

These things said he: and after that he saith unto them, our friend Lazarus sleepeth; but I go, that I may awake him out of sleep.

Then said his disciples, Lord, if he sleep, he shall do well.

Howbeit Jesus spoke of his death: but they thought that he had spoken of taking of rest in sleep.

Then said Jesus unto them plainly, Lazarus is dead.

And I am glad for your sakes that I was not there, to the intent ye may believe; nevertheless let us go unto him.

Then said Thomas, which is called Didymus, unto his fellow disciples, let us also go, that we may die with him.

Then when Jesus came, he found that he had lain in the grave four days already.

Now Bethany was nigh unto Jerusalem, about fifteen furlongs off:

And many of the Jews came to Martha and Mary, to comfort them concerning their brother.

Then Martha, as soon as she heard that Jesus was coming, went and met him: but Mary sat still in the house.

Then said Martha unto Jesus, Lord, if thou hadst been here, my brother had not died.

But I know, that even now, whatsoever thou wilt ask of God, God will give it thee.

Jesus saith unto her, thy brother shall rise again.

Martha saith unto him, I know that he shall rise again in the resurrection at the last day.

Jesus said unto her, I am the resurrection, and the life: he that believeth in me, though he were dead, yet shall he live:

And whosoever liveth and believeth in me shall never die. Believest thou this?

She saith unto him, Yea, Lord: I believe that thou art the Christ, the Son of God, which should come into the world.

And when she had so said, she went her way, and called Mary her sister secretly, saying, The Master is come, and calleth for thee.

As soon as she heard that, she arose quickly, and came unto him.

Now Jesus was not yet come into the town but was in that place where Martha met him.

The Jews then which were with her in the house, and comforted her, when they saw Mary, that she rose up hastily and went out, followed her, saying, she goeth unto the grave to weep there.

Then when Mary was come where Jesus was, and saw him, she fell down at his feet, saying unto him, Lord, if thou hadst been here, my brother had not died.

When Jesus therefore saw her weeping, and the Jews also weeping which came with her, he groaned in the spirit, and was troubled.

And said, where have ye laid him? They said unto him, Lord, come and see. Jesus wept.

Then said the Jews, behold how he loved him!

And some of them said, could not this man, which opened the eyes of the blind, have caused that even this man should not have died?

Jesus therefore again groaning in himself cometh to the grave. It was a cave, and a stone lay upon it.

Jesus said, Take ye away the stone. Martha, the sister of him that was dead, saith unto him, Lord, by this time he stinketh: for he hath been dead four days.

Jesus saith unto her, Said I not unto thee, that, if thou wouldest believe, thou shouldest see the glory of God?

Then they took away the stone from the place where the dead was laid. And Jesus lifted up his eyes, and said, Father, I thank thee that thou hast heard me.

And I knew that thou hearest me always: but because of the people which stand by I said it, that they may believe that thou hast sent me.

And when he thus had spoken, he cried with a loud voice, Lazarus, come forth.

And he that was dead came forth, bound hand and foot with graveclothes: and his face was bound about with a napkin. Jesus saith unto them, loose him, and let him go.

Then many of the Jews which came to Mary, and had seen the things which Jesus did, believed on him. But some of them went their ways to the Pharisees and told them what things Jesus had done.
(John 11: 1-46 KJV)

Jesus Speaks A Third Time About His Death

Then he took unto him the twelve, and said unto them, Behold, we go up to Jerusalem, and all things that are written by the prophets concerning the Son of man shall be accomplished.

For he shall be delivered unto the Gentiles, and shall be mocked, and spitefully entreated, and spitted on:

And they shall scourge him and put him to death: and the third day he shall rise again. And they understood none of these things: and this saying was hid from them, neither knew they the things which were spoken. (Luke 18: 31-34 KJV)

A Mother's Request

Then came to him the mother of Zebedees children with her sons, worshipping him, and desiring a certain thing of him.

And he said unto her, what wilt thou? She saith unto him, Grant that these my two sons may sit, the one on thy right hand, and the other on the left, in thy kingdom.

But Jesus answered and said, Ye know not what ye ask. Are ye able to drink of the cup that I shall drink of, and to be baptized with the baptism that I am baptized with? They say unto him, we are able.

And he saith unto them, Ye shall drink indeed of my cup, and be baptized with the baptism that I am baptized with but to sit on my right hand, and on my left, is not mine to give, but it shall be given to them for whom it is prepared of my Father.

And when the ten heard it, they were moved with indignation against the two brethren.

But Jesus called them unto him, and said, Ye know that the princes of the Gentiles exercise dominion over them, and they that are great exercise authority upon them.

But it shall not be so among you: but whosoever will be great among you, let him be your minister; And whosoever will be chief among you, let him be your servant: Even as the Son of man came not to be ministered unto, but to minister, and to give his life a ransom for many. (Matthew: 20: 20-28 KJV)

Focus Questions

1	What lesson is learned from the parable of the workers in the vineyard?	3	How many times did Jesus speak about his death?
2	Why did the Jewish authorities want to kill Jesus?	4	What did Jesus tell the apostles that he came down to the earth for?

Note:

Much of what happened to Jesus seems to have come about 'to fulfil the prophesy', and when explained in that context it is much easier to come to terms with the events. Perhaps this is how we are meant to view events in our own lives – instead of agonizing over why our lives take the directions they do, accepting that there is an underlying reason (that we may not comprehend at the time) leads to a sense of calm and purpose that is missing in our lives a lot of the time.

Reflection

After a tragedy happens to us or to one of our loved ones, we realize that we had no control over it and we may go through a great pain of mind. If we trust God and accept his Will, would we not become strong to cope with any tragedy that befalls us?

Chapter 24
Jesus on His Way to Jerusalem

Events that took place when Jesus was travelling to Jerusalem is considered in this chapter.

Learning Outcome

- know what happened to Bartimaeus and Zacchaeus
- know why Jesus was impressed by Martha's anointing

Jesus Heals Blind Bartimaeus (Miracle 32)

And they came to Jericho: and as he went out of Jericho with his disciples and a great number of people, blind Bartimaeus, the son of Timaeus, sat by the highway side begging.

And when he heard that it was Jesus of Nazareth, he began to cry out, and say, Jesus, thou son of David, have mercy on me.

And many charged him that he should hold his peace: but he cried the more a great deal, thou son of David, have mercy on me.

And Jesus stood still and commanded him to be called. And they call the blind man, saying unto him, be of good comfort, rise; he calleth thee.

And he, casting away his garment, rose, and came to Jesus.

185

And Jesus answered and said unto him, what wilt thou that I should do unto thee? The blind man said unto him, Lord, that I might receive my sight.

And Jesus said unto him, go thy way; thy faith hath made thee whole. And immediately he received his sight, and followed Jesus in the way (Mark: 10: 46-52 KJV)

Jesus and Zacchaeus

And Jesus entered and passed through Jericho.

And, behold, there was a man named Zacchaeus, which was the chief among the publicans, and he was rich.

And he sought to see Jesus who he was; and could not for the press, because he was little of stature.

And he ran before and climbed up into a sycomore tree to see him: for he was to pass that way.

And when Jesus came to the place, he looked up, and saw him, and said unto him, Zacchaeus, make haste, and come down; for today I must abide at thy house.

And he made haste, and came down, and received him joyfully.

And when they saw it, they all murmured, saying, that he was gone to be guest with a man that is a sinner.

And Zacchaeus stood, and said unto the Lord: Behold, Lord, the half of my goods I give to the poor; and if I have taken anything from any man by false accusation, I restore him fourfold.

And Jesus said unto him, this day is salvation come to this house, for so much as he also is a son of Abraham.

For the Son of man is come to seek and to save that which was lost. (Luke 19: 1-10 KJV)

The Parable of the Three Servants (Parable 26)

For the kingdom of heaven is as a man travelling into a far country, who called his own servants, and delivered unto them his goods.

And unto one he gave five talents, to another two, and to another one; to every man according to his several ability; and straightway took his journey.

Then he that had received the five talents went and traded with the same and made them other five talents.

And likewise, he that had received two, he also gained other two.

But he that had received one went and digged in the earth and hid his lord's money.

After a long time, the lord of those servants cometh, and reckoneth with them.

And so, he that had received five talents came and brought other five talents, saying, Lord, thou deliveredst unto me five talents: behold, I have gained beside them five talents more.

His lord said unto him, Well done, thou good and faithful servant: thou hast been faithful over a few things, I will make thee ruler over many things: enter thou into the joy of thy lord.

He also that had received two talents came and said, Lord, thou deliveredst unto me two talents: behold, I have gained two other talents beside them.

His lord said unto him, Well done, good and faithful servant; thou hast been faithful over a few things, I will make thee ruler over many things: enter thou into the joy of thy lord.

Then he which had received the one talent came and said, Lord, I knew thee that thou art an hard man, reaping where thou hast not sown, and gathering where thou hast not strawed:

And I was afraid and went and hid thy talent in the earth: lo, there thou hast that is thine.

His lord answered and said unto him, thou wicked and slothful servant, thou knewest that I reap where I sowed not, and gather where I have not strawed:

Thou oughtest therefore to have put my money to the exchangers, and then at my coming I should have received mine own with usury.

Take therefore the talent from him and give it unto him which hath ten talents.

For unto everyone that hath shall be given, and he shall have abundance: but from him that hath not shall be taken away even that which he hath.

And cast ye the unprofitable servant into outer darkness: there shall be weeping and gnashing of teeth.
(Matthew: 25: 14-30 KJV)

Broadly speaking, the word 'talent' can be used to all of the various gifts God has given us for our use, which includes all gifts natural, spiritual, and material.

One of the simplest lessons from this parable is that it is not immoral to profit from our resources, wit, and labor.

God wants us to use our talents towards productive ends. The parable emphasizes the need for work and creativity, as opposed to idleness.

Jesus is Anointed at Bethany

Now when Jesus was in Bethany, in the house of Simon the leper,

There came unto him a woman having an alabaster box of very precious ointment, and poured it on his head, as he sat at meat.

But when his disciples saw it, they had indignation, saying, to what purpose is this waste?

For this ointment might have been sold for much and given to the poor.

When Jesus understood it, he said unto them, why trouble ye the woman? for she hath wrought a good work upon me.

For ye have the poor always with you; but me ye have not always.

For in that she hath poured this ointment on my body, she did it for my burial.

Verily I say unto you, wheresoever this gospel shall be preached in the whole world, there shall also this, that this woman hath done, be told for a memorial of her.
(Matthew: 26: 6-13 KJV)

Focus Questions

1	What words did Jesus say before he made Bartimaeus to see again?	3	What lesson is to be learned from the parable of the three servants?
2	What did Zacchaeus tell Jesus?	4	What did Jesus say was the significance of Martha anointing him?

Note:

If the hidden meaning is not apparent, the parable of the three servants would cause confusion in the reader's mind. On the one hand, the parable can be taken as advocating judicious use of our 'talents', which is a useful principle for us. God can question our inability to use the talents and skills he has given us, to serve his people as well as to help ourselves. So, we must do our best to use them.

On the other hand, the parable can be misconstrued as saying that God is harsh and unforgiving, punishing the third servant simply for being lazy. One could then ask; would it not be better for the master to counsel the servant about his fears and help him utilize his 'talent'? One could also ask; would we not be better off by a belief in a benevolent God who will support us despite our failures and human fears?

Reflection

Different people have different needs at different times. Jesus will certainly help us out if we cry out to him like Bartimaeus did. Therefore, should we not always think that Jesus is asking "What do you want me to do for you?"

Chapter 25
Jesus in Jerusalem

Jesus enters Jerusalem to fulfil his Father's will.

Learning Outcome

- know the events that happened as Jesus entered Jerusalem to face his impending death.

The Triumphant Entry into Jerusalem

And when they drew nigh unto Jerusalem, and were come to Bethphage, unto the mount of Olives, then sent Jesus two disciples,

Saying unto them, go into the village over against you, and straightway ye shall find an ass tied, and a colt with her: loose them, and bring them unto me.

And if any man say ought unto you, ye shall say, The Lord hath need of them; and straightway he will send them.

All this was done, that it might be fulfilled which was spoken by the prophet, saying,

Tell ye the daughter of Sion, Behold, thy King cometh unto thee, meek, and sitting upon an ass, and a colt the foal of an ass.

And the disciples went, and did as Jesus commanded them,

And brought the ass, and the colt, and put on them their clothes, and they set him thereon.

And a very great multitude spread their garments in the way; others cut down branches from the trees, and strawed them in the way.

And the multitudes that went before, and that followed, cried, saying, Hosanna to the son of David: Blessed is he that cometh in the name of the Lord; Hosanna in the highest.

And when he was come into Jerusalem, all the city was moved, saying, who is this?

And the multitude said, this is Jesus the prophet of Nazareth of Galilee. (Matthew: 21: 1-11 KJV)

Jesus Weeps Over Jerusalem

And when he was come near, he beheld the city, and wept over it,

Saying, if thou hadst known, even thou, at least in this thy day, the things which belong unto thy peace! but now they are hid from thine eyes.

For the days shall come upon thee, that thine enemies shall cast a trench about thee, and compass thee round, and keep thee in on every side,

And shall lay thee even with the ground, and thy children within thee; and they shall not leave in thee one stone upon another; because thou knewest not the time of thy visitation.
(Luke 19: 41-44 KJV)

Jesus in The Temple

And Jesus went into the temple of God, and cast out all them that sold and bought in the temple, and overthrew the tables of the moneychangers, and the seats of them that sold doves,

And said unto them, It is written, My house shall be called the house of prayer; but ye have made it a den of thieves.

And the blind and the lame came to him in the temple; and he healed them.

And when the chief priests and scribes saw the wonderful things that he did, and the children crying in the temple, and saying, Hosanna to the son of David; they were sore displeased,

And said unto him, Hearest thou what these say? And Jesus saith unto them, Yea; have ye never read, Out of the mouth of babes and sucklings thou hast perfected praise?
(Matthew 21: 12-16 KJV)

Some Greeks Seek Jesus

And there were certain Greeks among them that came up to worship at the feast:

The same came therefore to Philip, which was of Bethsaida of Galilee, and desired him, saying, Sir, we would see Jesus.

Philip cometh and telleth Andrew: and again, Andrew and Philip tell Jesus.

And Jesus answered them, saying, the hour is come, that the Son of man should be glorified.

Verily, verily, I say unto you, except a corn of wheat fall into the ground and die, it abideth alone: but if it die, it bringeth forth much fruit.

He that loveth his life shall lose it; and he that hateth his life in this world shall keep it unto life eternal.

If any man serve me, let him follow me; and where I am, there shall also my servant be: if any man serve me, him will my Father honour.
(John 12: 20-26 KJV)

The Voice from Heaven

Now is my soul troubled; and what shall I say? Father save me from this hour: but for this cause came I unto this hour.

Father glorify thy name. Then came there a voice from heaven, saying, I have both glorified it, and will glorify it again.

The people, therefore, that stood by, and heard it, said that it thundered: others said, An angel spoke to him.

Jesus answered and said, this voice came not because of me, but for your sakes.

Now is the judgment of this world: now shall the prince of this world be cast out.

And I, if I be lifted up from the earth, will draw all men unto me.

This he said, signifying what death he should die.
(John 12: 27-33 KJV)

Who is this Son of Man?

The people answered him, we have heard out of the law that Christ abideth for ever: and how sayest thou, The Son of man must be lifted up? who is this Son of man?

Then Jesus said unto them, yet a little while is the light with you. Walk while ye have the light, lest darkness come upon you: for he that walketh in darkness knoweth not whither he goeth.

While ye have light, believe in the light, that ye may be the children of light. These things spoke Jesus, and departed, and did hide himself from them.
(John 12: 34-36 KJV)

Jesus Curses the Fig Tree (Miracle 33)

Now in the morning as he returned into the city, he hungered.

And when he saw a fig tree in the way, he came to it, and found nothing thereon, but leaves only, and said unto it, let no fruit grow on thee henceforward forever. And presently the fig tree withered away.

And when the disciples saw it, they marveled, saying, how soon is the fig tree withered away!

Jesus answered and said unto them, Verily I say unto you, if ye have faith, and doubt not, ye shall not only do this which is done to the fig tree, but also if ye shall say unto this mountain, Be thou removed, and be thou cast into the sea; it shall be done.

And all things, whatsoever ye shall ask in prayer, believing, ye shall receive.
(Matthew 21: 18-22 KJV)

Focus Questions

1	What kind of reception did Jesus receive when he entered Jerusalem?	3	What did Jesus say about prayer?
2	What did Jesus do when he went to the Temple in Jerusalem?	4	What did Jesus say will happen to those who serve him?

Note:

What did Jesus mean when he said, "Those who love their own life will lose it; those who hate their own life in this world will keep it for life eternal"? Are we not supposed to value our lives, a great gift from God, and our bodies which are our 'temples'; is suicide not a mortal sin because it is the equivalent of destroying God's gift to us?

Jesus was only warning about excessive love for life that could lead us in the wrong paths.

And why did Jesus curse the fruitless fig tree instead of performing the reverse miracle to make it bear fruit endlessly? The fig tree was created for a purpose and the tree did not do what it was intended to do. The parable was to illustrate God's concern when his chosen people failed to deliver his expectations.

If we believe, and receive whatever we ask for in prayer (as Jesus said), should we not refrain from knowingly asking for things that are selfish and are not in the best interest of our fellow human beings?

Reflection

God created us to praise and glorify him with all what we do in our lives. He is always with us, helping us when we do things by completely following his teachings. He is there with us every step of the way grooming us for his kingdom.

Chapter 26
Parables of Jesus in Jerusalem

Jesus teaches through parables in Jerusalem.

Learning Outcome

- Know the true meaning of the parables in this chapter.

The Elders Question Jesus's Authority

And when he was come into the temple, the chief priests and the elders of the people came unto him as he was teaching, and said, By what authority doest thou these things? and who gave thee this authority?

And Jesus answered and said unto them, I also will ask you one thing, which if ye tell me, I in likewise will tell you by what authority I do these things.

The baptism of John, whence was it? from heaven, or of men? And they reasoned with themselves, saying, If we shall say, From heaven; he will say unto us, Why did ye not then believe him?

But if we shall say, of men; we fear the people; for all hold John as a prophet.

And they answered Jesus, and said, we cannot tell. And he said unto them, neither tell I you by what authority I do these things.
(Matthew 21: 23-27 KJV)

The Parable of the Two Sons (Parable 27)

Jesus told this parable:

But what think ye? A certain man had two sons; and he came to the first, and said, Son, go work today in my vineyard.

He answered and said, I will not: but afterward he repented, and went.

And he came to the second and said likewise. And he answered and said, I go, sir: and went not.

Whether of them twain did the will of his father? They say unto him, The first. Jesus saith unto them, Verily I say unto you, That the publicans and the harlots go into the kingdom of God before you.

For John came unto you in the way of righteousness, and ye believed him not: but the publicans and the harlots believed him: and ye, when ye had seen it, repented not afterward, that ye might believe him.
(Matthew 21: 28-32 KJV)

The Tenants in The Vineyard (Parable 28)

Hear another parable: There was a certain householder, which planted a vineyard, and hedged it round about, and digged a winepress in it, and built a tower, and let it out to husbandmen, and went into a far country:

And when the time of the fruit drew near, he sent his servants to the husbandmen, that they might receive the fruits of it.

And the husbandmen took his servants, and beat one, and killed another, and stoned another.

Again, he sent other servants more than the first: and they did unto them likewise.

But last of all he sent unto them his son, saying, they will reverence my son.

But when the husbandmen saw the son, they said among themselves, this is the heir; come, let us kill him, and let us seize on his inheritance.

And they caught him, and cast him out of the vineyard, and slew him.

When the lord therefore of the vineyard cometh, what will he do unto those husbandmen?

They say unto him, He will miserably destroy those wicked men, and will let out his vineyard unto other husbandmen, which shall render him the fruits in their seasons.
(Matthew 21: 33-41 KJV)

The land owner represents God, the vineyard his kingdom, the tenants are the Israel's religious leaders and all who reject him, the servants are God's prophets and faithful believers, and the beloved son is Jesus.

Rejected Stone Becomes the Corner Stone (Parable 29)

Jesus saith unto them, did ye never read in the scriptures, The stone which the builders rejected, the same is become the head of the corner: this is the Lord's doing, and it is marvelous in our eyes?

Therefore, say I unto you, the kingdom of God shall be taken from you, and given to a nation bringing forth the fruits thereof.

And whosoever shall fall on this stone shall be broken but on whomsoever it shall fall, it will grind him to powder.
(Matthew 21: 42-44; KJV)

A stone at the corner of a building uniting two intersecting walls is the corner stone. The stone is Jesus.

Elevation of the stone as corner stone is the resurrection of Jesus.

The builders are the rulers of the people and elders.

The rejection of the stone is the crucifixion of Jesus.

The resurrection declares that Jesus is the Son of God in power.

Humility and Hospitality (Parable 30)

And he put forth a parable to those which were bidden, when he marked how they chose out the chief rooms; saying unto them,

When thou art bidden of any man to a wedding, sit not down in the highest room; lest a more honorable man than thou be bidden of him;

And he that bade thee and him come and say to thee, Give this man place; and thou begin with shame to take the lowest room.

But when thou art bidden, go and sit down in the lowest room; that when he that bade thee cometh, he may say unto thee, Friend, go up higher: then shalt thou have worship in the presence of them that sit at meat with thee.

For whosoever exalteth himself shall be abased; and he that humbleth himself shall be exalted.
(Luke 14: 7-11 KJV)

By providing instruction about attending functions on earth Jesus is making us think about how to become worthy to be at the banquet feast which has no end. He wants us to humble ourselves in this life to be eligible to get exalted in the eternal life with him.

The Parable of the Wedding Feast (Parable 31)

The kingdom of heaven is like unto a certain king, which made a marriage for his son, And sent forth his servants to call them that were bidden to the wedding: and they would not come.

Again, he sent forth other servants, saying, tell them which are bidden, Behold, I have prepared my dinner: my oxen and my fatlings are killed, and all things are ready: come unto the marriage.

But they made light of it, and went their ways, one to his farm, another to his merchandise:

And the remnant took his servants, and entreated them spitefully, and slew them.

But when the king heard thereof, he was wroth: and he sent forth his armies, and destroyed those murderers, and burned up their city.

Then saith he to his servants, the wedding is ready, but they which were bidden were not worthy.

Go ye therefore into the highways, and as many as ye shall find, bid to the marriage.

So those servants went out into the highways, and gathered together all as many as they found, both bad and good: and the wedding was furnished with guests.

And when the king came in to see the guests, he saw there a man which had not on a wedding garment:

And he saith unto him, Friend, how camest thou in hither not having a wedding garment? And he was speechless.

Then said the king to the servants, bind him hand and foot, and take him away, and cast him into outer darkness, there shall be weeping and gnashing of teeth. For many are called, but few are chosen.
(Matthew 22: 2-14 KJV)

The Israelites were invited to be the honored guests in the Kingdom of Heaven. They refused to accept the invitation and so others were invited. A wedding garment is provided by the king, and it is an insult to him if a person does not wear it. The person who failed to wear the wedding garment represents a Christian in name only. The garment represents the salvation to be found in Jesus by his death on the cross. This parable's message is that we must rely on God's provision of salvation and not on our own good works and services.

God calls everyone and gives them the power to respond—but to be chosen, we must respond to the call, using the power God gave us for that purpose.

Faithful or the Unfaithful Servant (Parable 32)

Who then is a faithful and wise servant, whom his lord hath made ruler over his household, to give them meat in due season?

Blessed is that servant, whom his lord when he cometh shall find so doing.

Verily I say unto you, that he shall make him ruler over all his goods.

But and if that evil servant shall say in his heart, My lord delayeth his coming; And shall begin to smite his fellow servants, and to eat and drink with the drunken;

The lord of that servant shall come in a day when he looketh not for him, and in an hour that he is not aware of,

And shall cut him asunder and appoint him his portion with the hypocrites: there shall be weeping and gnashing of teeth.
(Matthew 24: 45-51 KJV)

This is one of several parables that reveal the structure and ruler-ship of the kingdom of heaven. A king is not effective unless his subjects obey him. There is a kingdom in heaven where God, the Father, is the King and the citizens there obey his instructions. God wants his instructions to be obeyed here on earth in the same way as they are obeyed in heaven!

Focus Questions

1	What reply did Jesus given when he was asked '"What right do you have to do these things? Who gave you such right?"	4	What do you understand by the saying 'the rejected stone becomes the corner stone'?
2	What lesson is learned from the parable of the two sons?	5	Which parable says that we must depend on the salvation God provides?
3	What does the parable of the tenants in the vineyard teach us?	6	Who is a faithful and wise servant?

Note:

Unless one does the Will of God, he or she cannot enter the Kingdom of God. What then is the Will of God? The Will of God is what God inspires us to do in our daily life for the good of humanity rather than acting selfishly for our own ends. God wants to make us more like Jesus so He can use us for His Will.

Reflection

A contrite heart and humble spirit will help us to know the Will of God, but this alone will not help us to enter the kingdom of God. The vital ingredients are our actions that are in conformity with His commandments.

Chapter 27
Jesus Answers Tricky Questions

This chapter considers what Jesus told about the end of the world.

Learning Outcome

- know how the Pharisees tried to frame Jesus.
- know the signs Jesus said to expect before the end of the world.

The Question About Paying Taxes

Then went the Pharisees and took counsel how they might entangle him in his talk.

And they sent out unto him their disciples with the Herodians, saying, Master, we know that thou art true, and teachest the way of God in truth, neither carest thou for any man: for thou regardest not the person of men.

Tell us therefore, What thinkest thou? Is it lawful to give tribute unto Caesar, or not?

But Jesus perceived their wickedness, and said, why tempt ye me, ye hypocrites?

Shew me the tribute money. And they brought unto him a penny.

And he saith unto them, whose is this image and superscription?

They say unto him, Caesar's. Then saith he unto them, render therefore unto Caesar the things which are Caesar's; and unto God the things that are God's.

When they had heard these words, they marveled, and left him, and went their way.
(Matthew 22: 15 - 22 KJV)

The Question About Rising from Death

The same day came to him the Sadducees, which say that there is no resurrection, and asked him,

Saying, Master, Moses said, If a man dies, having no children, his brother shall marry his wife, and raise up seed unto his brother.

Now there were with us seven brethren: and the first, when he had married a wife, deceased, and, having no issue, left his wife unto his brother:

Likewise, the second also, and the third, unto the seventh.

And last of all the woman died also.

Therefore, in the resurrection whose wife shall she be of the seven? for they all had her.

Jesus answered and said unto them, Ye do err, not knowing the scriptures, nor the power of God.

For in the resurrection they neither marry, nor are given in marriage, but are as the angels of God in heaven.

But as touching the resurrection of the dead, have ye not read that which was spoken unto you by God, saying,

I am the God of Abraham, and the God of Isaac, and the God of Jacob? God is not the God of the dead, but of the living.

And when the multitude heard this, they were astonished at his doctrine. (Matthew 22: 23 - 33 KJV)

The Widow's Offering

And he looked up, and saw the rich men casting their gifts into the treasury. And he saw also a certain poor widow casting in thither two mites.

And he said, of a truth I say unto you, that this poor widow hath cast in more than they all:

For all these have of their abundance cast in unto the offerings of God: but she of her penury hath cast in all the living that she had. (Luke 21: 1- 4 KJV)

Jesus Speaks of The Destruction of Jerusalem

And Jesus went out and departed from the temple: and his disciples came to him for to shew him the buildings of the temple. And Jesus said unto them, see ye not all these things? verily I say unto you, There shall not be left here one stone upon another, that shall not be thrown down. (Matthew 24: 1-2 KJV)

Troubles and Persecution

And as he sat upon the mount of Olives, the disciples came unto him privately, saying, tell us, when shall these things be? and what shall be the sign of thy coming, and of the end of the world?

And Jesus answered and said unto them, take heed that no man deceive you.

For many shall come in my name, saying, I am Christ; and shall deceive many.

And ye shall hear of wars and rumors of wars: see that ye be not troubled: for all these things must come to pass, but the end is not yet.

For nation shall rise against nation, and kingdom against kingdom: and there shall be famines, and pestilences, and earthquakes, in divers' places.

All these are the beginning of sorrows.

Then shall they deliver you up to be afflicted and shall kill you: and ye shall be hated of all nations for my name's sake.

And then shall many be offended, and shall betray one another, and shall hate one another.

And many false prophets shall rise and shall deceive many.

And because iniquity shall abound, the love of many shall wax cold.

But he that shall endure unto the end, the same shall be saved.

And this gospel of the kingdom shall be preached in all the world for a witness unto all nations; and then shall the end come.
(Matthew 24: 3-14 KJV)

The Awful Horror

When ye therefore shall see the abomination of desolation, spoken of by Daniel the prophet, stand in the holy place, (whoso readeth, let him understand:)

Then let them which be in Judaea flee into the mountains:

Let him which is on the housetop not come down to take anything out of his house:

Neither let him which is in the field return back to take his clothes.

And woe unto them that are with child, and to them that give suck in those days!

But pray ye that your flight be not in the winter, neither on the sabbath day:

For then shall be great tribulation, such as was not since the beginning of the world to this time, no, nor ever shall be.

And except those days should be shortened, there should no flesh be saved: but for the elect's sake those days shall be shortened.
(Matthew 24: 15-22 KJV)

The Coming of the Son of Man

Immediately after the tribulation of those days shall the sun be darkened, and the moon shall not give her light, and the stars shall fall from heaven, and the powers of the heavens shall be shaken:

And then shall appear the sign of the Son of man in heaven: and then shall all the tribes of the earth mourn, and they shall see the Son of man coming in the clouds of heaven with power and great glory.

And he shall send his angels with a great sound of a trumpet, and they shall gather together his elect from the four winds, from one end of heaven to the other.
(Matthew 24: 29-31 KJV)

The Lesson of the Fig Tree

Now learn a parable of the fig tree; When his branch is yet tender, and putteth forth leaves, ye know that summer is nigh:

So likewise, ye, when ye shall see all these things, know that it is near, even at the doors.

Verily I say unto you, this generation shall not pass, till all these things be fulfilled.

Heaven and earth shall pass away, but my words shall not pass away.
(Matthew 24: 32-35 KJV)

The Need to Watch

And take heed to yourselves, lest at any time your hearts be overcharged with surfeiting, and drunkenness, and cares of this life, and so that day come upon you unawares.

For as a snare shall it come on all them that dwell on the face of the whole earth.

Watch ye therefore, and pray always, that ye may be accounted worthy to escape all these things that shall come to pass, and to stand before the Son of man.
(Luke 21: 34-36 KJV)

And this know, that if the good man of the house had known what hour the thief would come, he would have watched, and not have suffered his house to be broken through.

Be ye therefore ready also: for the Son of man cometh at an hour when ye think not.
(Luke 12: 39-40 KJV)

Focus Questions

1	What answer did Jesus give when he was asked "Is it against our Law to pay taxes to the Roman Emperor or not?"	3	What signs did Jesus say would people see before the end of the world?
2	What answer did Jesus give when asked 'Who will be the husband of a woman who married seven brothers when the dead rise to life?	4	When did Jesus say the world will end with the Son of man coming again?

Note:

We try to be on our best behavior in order to gain a reward, but we find that it is very difficult to maintain behavior that is not natural to us without truly believing in the need for that behavior. Similarly, it will certainly be difficult for us to live our whole life in the way Jesus taught, if we are only doing it because of the promise of eternal life in the Kingdom of God.

The people who succeed in living the way Jesus preached could be identified as the ones who see the benefit for their fellow humans and do not only concern themselves with what they may attain for themselves by the way they live.

Reflection

In practical terms, on an individual level, the end of the world could represent our death, an event that is entirely unpredictable. In order to be always prepared for this event, should we not allow the principles of Jesus to become our principles, and his spirit to become the source of inspiration for our daily lives?

Chapter 28
The Final Judgement

This chapter looks at what Jesus told about the final judgment.

Learning Outcome

- Know what Jesus said about how we will be judged at the end of the world.

The Parable of the Ten Young Women (Parable 33)

Then shall the kingdom of heaven be likened unto ten virgins, which took their lamps, and went forth to meet the bridegroom.

And five of them were wise, and five were foolish.

They that were foolish took their lamps, and took no oil with them:

But the wise took oil in their vessels with their lamps.

While the bridegroom tarried, they all slumbered and slept.

And at midnight there was a cry made, Behold, the bridegroom cometh; go ye out to meet him.

Then all those virgins arose and trimmed their lamps.

And the foolish said unto the wise, give us of your oil; for our lamps are gone out.

But the wise answered, saying, not so; lest there be not enough for us and you: but go ye rather to them that sell, and buy for yourselves.

And while they went to buy, the bridegroom came; and they that were ready went in with him to the marriage: and the door was shut.

Afterward came also the other virgins, saying, Lord, Lord, open to us.

But he answered and said, Verily I say unto you, I know you not.

Watch therefore, for ye know neither the day nor the hour wherein the Son of man cometh.
(Matthew 25: 1-13 KJV)

The bridegroom is Jesus. The bridesmaids represent people on earth during the Great Disturbances that would take place in the last days. The bridesmaids with oil represent those who will have given their hearts to Jesus and who are alert for His second coming. Those without oil are those who haven't given their hearts to Jesus and who are not ready for the coming of Jesus. Those who gave their hearts to him and waited for Him will only be allowed into the Kingdom of heaven and others will be denied entrance.

This parable gives the clearest warning to those whom Jesus would find still on earth when he returns, to make sure that they are ready to receive him.

He will find both who have done the will of God and those who refused to do the will of God.

Eternal Life or Eternal Punishment

When the Son of man shall come in his glory, and all the holy angels with him, then shall he sit upon the throne of his glory:

And before him shall be gathered all nations: and he shall separate them one from another, as a shepherd divideth his sheep from the goats:

And he shall set the sheep on his right hand, but the goats on the left.

Then shall the King say unto them on his right hand, Come, ye blessed of my Father, inherit the kingdom prepared for you from the foundation of the world:

For I was an hungred, and ye gave me meat: I was thirsty, and ye gave me drink: I was a stranger, and ye took me in:

Naked, and ye clothed me: I was sick, and ye visited me: I was in prison, and ye came unto me.

Then shall the righteous answer him, saying, Lord, when saw we thee an hungred, and fed thee? or thirsty, and gave thee drink?

When saw we thee a stranger, and took thee in? or naked, and clothed thee?

Or when saw we thee sick, or in prison, and came unto thee?

And the King shall answer and say unto them, Verily I say unto you, In as much as ye have done it unto one of the least of these my brethren, ye have done it unto me.

Then shall he say also unto them on the left hand, depart from me, ye cursed, into everlasting fire, prepared for the devil and his angels:

For I was an hungred, and ye gave me no meat: I was thirsty, and ye gave me no drink:

I was a stranger, and ye took me not in: naked, and ye clothed me not: sick, and in prison, and ye visited me not.

Then shall they also answer him, saying, Lord, when saw we thee an hungred, or athirst, or a stranger, or naked, or sick, or in prison, and did not minister unto thee?

Then shall he answer them, saying, Verily I say unto you, in as much as ye did it not to one of the least of these, ye did it not to me.

And these shall go away into everlasting punishment: but the righteous into life eternal.
(Matthew 25: 31- 46 KJV)

Many will say to me in that day, Lord, Lord, have we not prophesied in thy name? and in thy name have cast out devils? and in thy name done many wonderful works?

And then will I profess unto them*, I never knew you: depart from me, ye that work iniquity.
(Matthew 7: 22- 23 KJV)

Focus Questions

1	What do we learn from the parable of the ten young women?	2	What did Jesus say about how the final judgment will take place?

Note:

The words of Jesus about how we treat the 'least important' of our fellow humans are powerful. Was he referring to the people that society considers unimportant because of their social status or apparent lack of contribution to society? Even if we could decide on who those people might be, what gives us the right to make that distinction except for the arbitrary rules that are formed in society?

The people Jesus refers to as "hungry, thirsty, naked, etc." are people who needed our utmost attention. If we have neglected these brothers and sisters in our life, do we really qualify to enter eternal life?

Reflection

Jesus, living in each of us, can make a difference in the world. He teaches us that we could achieve this by seeing his face in our brothers and sisters.

Chapter 29
The Time Nears for Jesus's Death

This chapter considers the events that took place before Jesus was betrayed.

Learning Outcome

- know how Judas betrayed Jesus
- know where Jesus and his disciples ate the Passover meal
- know what happened when Jesus was washing the disciples' feet
- know the significance of the last supper
- know what Jesus predicted about his betrayal by Judas and denial by Peter.

A Samaritan Village Refuses to Receive Jesus

Now it came to pass, when the time had come for Him to be received up, that He steadfastly set His face to go to Jerusalem and sent messengers before His face.

And as they went, they entered a village of the Samaritans, to prepare for Him.

But they did not receive Him, because His face was set for the journey to Jerusalem.

And when His disciples James and John saw this, they said, "Lord, do You want us to command fire to come down from heaven and consume them, just as Elijah did?"

But He turned and rebuked them, and said, "You do not know what manner of spirit you are of. For the Son of Man did not come to destroy men's lives but to save them." And they went to another village (Luke 9: 51-56 KJV)

The Plot Against Jesus

And it came to pass, when Jesus had finished all these sayings, he said unto his disciples,

Ye know that after two days is the feast of the passover, and the Son of man is betrayed to be crucified.

Then assembled together the chief priests, and the scribes, and the elders of the people, unto the palace of the high priest, who was called Caiaphas,

And consulted that they might take Jesus by subtilty and kill him.

But they said, not on the feast day, lest there be an uproar among the people.

Then one of the twelve, called Judas Iscariot, went unto the chief priests,

And said unto them, what will ye give me, and I will deliver him unto you? And they covenanted with him for thirty pieces of silver.

And from that time he sought opportunity to betray him. (Matthew 26: 1- 5, 14-16)

Jesus Prepares to Eat the Passover Meal

Then came the day of unleavened bread, when the passover must be killed.

And he sent Peter and John, saying, Go and prepare us the passover, that we may eat.

And they said unto him, where wilt thou that we prepare?

And he said unto them, Behold, when ye are entered into the city, there shall a man meet you, bearing a pitcher of water; follow him into the house where he entereth in.

And ye shall say unto the good man of the house, The Master saith unto thee, where is the guest chamber, where I shall eat the passover with my disciples?

And he shall shew you a large upper room furnished: there make ready.

And they went and found as he had said unto them: and they made ready the passover.
(Luke 22: 7-13 KJV)

And when the hour was come, he sat down, and the twelve apostles with him.

And he said unto them, with desire I have desired to eat this passover with you before I suffer:

For I say unto you, I will not any more eat thereof, until it be fulfilled in the kingdom of God.

And he took the cup, and gave thanks, and said, take this, and divide it among yourselves:

For I say unto you, I will not drink of the fruit of the vine, until the kingdom of God shall come.

And he took bread, and gave thanks, and broke it, and gave unto them, saying, this is my body which is given for you: this do in remembrance of me.

Likewise, also the cup after supper, saying, this cup is the new testament in my blood, which is shed for you.
(Luke 22: 14-20 KJV)

Jesus Washes His Disciples' Feet

He riseth from supper and laid aside his garments; and took a towel and girded himself. After that he poureth water into a basin, and began to wash the disciples' feet, and to wipe them with the towel wherewith he was girded.

Then cometh he to Simon Peter: and Peter saith unto him, Lord, dost thou wash my feet?

Jesus answered and said unto him, What I do thou knowest not now; but thou shalt know hereafter.

Peter saith unto him, thou shalt never wash my feet. Jesus answered him, If I wash thee not, thou hast no part with me.

Simon Peter saith unto him, Lord, not my feet only, but also my hands and my head.

Jesus saith to him, He that is washed needeth not save to wash his feet but is clean every whit: and ye are clean, but not all.

For he knew who should betray him; therefore, said he, Ye are not all clean.

So, after he had washed their feet, and had taken his garments, and was set down again, he said unto them, know what I have done to you?

Ye call me Master and Lord: and ye say well; for so I am.

If I then, your Lord and Master, have washed your feet; ye also ought to wash one another's feet.

For I have given you an example, that ye should do as I have done to you. (John 13: 4-19 KJV)

Jesus Predicts His Betrayal

And as they did eat, he said, Verily I say unto you, that one of you shall betray me.

And they were exceeding sorrowful, and began every one of them to say unto him, Lord, is it I?

And he answered and said, He that dippeth his hand with me in the dish, the same shall betray me.

The Son of man goeth as it is written of him: but woe unto that man by whom the Son of man is betrayed! it had been good for that man if he had not been born.

Then Judas, which betrayed him, answered and said, Master, is it I? He said unto him, thou hast said.

Now no man at the table knew for what intent he spoke this unto him.

For some of them thought, because Judas had the bag, that Jesus had said unto him, buy those things that we have need of against the feast; or, that he should give something to the poor.

He then having received the sop went immediately out: and it was night. (Matthew 26: 21-25; John 13: 28-30 KJV)

The Last Supper

And as they were eating, Jesus took bread, [a]blessed and broke it, and gave it to the disciples and said, "Take, eat; this is My body."

Then He took the cup, and gave thanks, and gave it to them, saying,

"Drink from it, all of you. For this is My blood of the new covenant, which is shed for many for the remission of sins.

But I say to you, I will not drink of this fruit of the vine from now on until that day when I drink it new with you in My Father's kingdom."

And when they had sung a hymn, they went out to the Mount of Olives. (Matthew 26: 26-30 KJV)

Jesus Predicts Peter's Denial

Then saith Jesus unto them, all ye shall be offended because of me this night: for it is written, I will smite the shepherd, and the sheep of the flock shall be scattered abroad.

But after I am risen again, I will go before you into Galilee.

Peter answered and said unto him, though all men shall be offended because of thee, yet will I never be offended.

Ye are they which have continued with me in my temptations.

And I appoint unto you a kingdom, as my Father hath appointed unto me;

That ye may eat and drink at my table in my kingdom and sit on thrones judging the twelve tribes of Israel.

And the Lord said, Simon, Simon, behold, Satan hath desired to have you, that he may sift you as wheat:

But I have prayed for thee, that thy faith fail not: and when thou art converted, strengthen thy brethren.

And he said unto him, Lord, I am ready to go with thee, both into prison, and to death.

And he said, I tell thee, Peter, the cock shall not crow this day, before that thou shalt thrice deny that thou knowest me.
(Matthew 26: 31-33; Luke 22: 28-34 KJV)

Focus Questions

1	For how many silver coins did Judas agree to betray Jesus?	4	What did Jesus say when Judas asked him "Surely, Teacher, you don't mean me?"
2	What was the venue for Jesus' Passover meal before his death?	5	What did Jesus say by raising the bread first and then the wine to heaven, during the last supper?
3	What happened between Jesus and Peter during the washing of the feet by Jesus?	6	What did Jesus say about Peter denying him?

Note:

This chapter contains some of the cornerstone events narrated in the bible to demonstrate Jesus' knowledge and awareness of what was to come. The issue of betrayal by Judas is interesting; this could be explained by saying that his actions were 'evil'. However, Peter's denial of Jesus makes things very puzzling. If the 'rock' could falter, then clearly this is a part of human nature, and therefore every one of us has the capacity to commit such a denial. Both Judas and Peter repented for their faults, but Peter asked for forgiveness. Sometimes we tend to call one person's action 'evil' and forgive another's 'betrayal'. This would seem somewhat hypocritical.

Our decision not to betray even if the reward for betrayal is significant, and our remorse if we have faltered, are the factors that would redeem us.

Reflection

Committing sin, feeling remorse and praying for forgiveness are all part of our lives. However, repeatedly and consciously committing sin and praying for forgiveness are a contradiction; it is a way of testing God's kindness for our pleasures and selfishness.

Chapter 30
Jesus's Return to His Father

Jesus tells his disciples that the time has come for him to return to his Father.

Learning Outcome

• know what Jesus said his disciples should do when he departs from them.

Sadness and Gladness

A little while, and ye shall not see me: and again, a little while, and ye shall see me, because I go to the Father.

Verily, verily, I say unto you, that ye shall weep and lament, but the world shall rejoice and ye shall be sorrowful, but your sorrow shall be turned into joy.

A woman when she is in travail hath sorrow, because her hour is come: but as soon as she is delivered of the child, she remembereth no more the anguish, for joy that a man is born into the world.

And ye now therefore have sorrow: but I will see you again, and your heart shall rejoice, and your joy no man taketh from you.
(John 16: 16, 20-22 KJV)

Jesus Speaks Openly

These things have I spoken unto you in proverbs: but the time cometh, when I shall no more speak unto you in proverbs, but I shall shew you plainly of the Father.

I came forth from the Father, and am come into the world: again, I leave the world, and go to the Father.

His disciples said unto him, Lo, now speakest thou plainly, and speakest no proverb.

Now are we sure that thou knowest all things, and needest not that any man should ask thee: by this we believe that thou camest forth from God.

Jesus answered them, do ye now believe?

Behold, the hour cometh, yea, is now come, that ye shall be scattered, every man to his own, and shall leave me alone: and yet I am not alone, because the Father is with me.

These things I have spoken unto you, that in me ye might have peace. In the world ye shall have tribulation: but be of good cheer; I have overcome the world.
(John 16: 25, 28-33 KJV)

There are two reasons for God to become a human. Firstly, by taking human nature and facing every trial and temptation imaginable, he restored a balance between good and evil. Secondly, by living the life he did and by his death and resurrection he glorified his humanity.

Purse, Bag and Sword

And he said unto them, When I sent you without purse, and scrip, and shoes, lacked ye anything? And they said, Nothing.

Then said he unto them, but now, he that hath a purse, let him take it, and likewise his scrip: and he that hath no sword, let him sell his garment, and buy one.

For I say unto you, that this that is written must yet be accomplished in me, and he was reckoned among the transgressors: for the things concerning me have an end.

And they said, Lord, behold, here are two swords. And he said unto them, it is enough.
(Luke 22: 35-38 KJV)

Jesus was speaking of the time when he sent the disciples out; they were then received well. Opposition to Jesus increased over three years and he knew that the situation was going to be different in the future. They must prepare to have the equipment for it. Jesus did not mean an actual sword. He was using the word to emphasize future danger. The apostles failed to understand Jesus. Peter showed him two swords. 'Enough!' does not mean that two swords among 11 apostles were enough. Jesus said it to end the conversation.

Focus Questions

1	With what did Jesus compare the apostles' sadness on his departure and the happiness on his reappearance?	2	What did Jesus mean when he said he has defeated the world?

Note:

Although Jesus is referring to his imminent suffering and death, his words about sadness turning into gladness may apply to many events in our lives. The disciples didn't know at the time that Jesus would be resurrected, but after the event they would have understood his words. Similarly, when faced with adverse times, we can choose to have faith that the meaning of the events will become clear to us eventually.

If we falter our faith, every event can potentially become overwhelming and take us to a point where our whole life seems meaningless and even unfair. Either way, it is a choice we make about how we perceive our life, so why not choose the option that will comfort us and give us strength?

Reflection

Everyone experiences difficulties in life, some minor and others unbearable. The Will of God for us does not impose suffering on us but if we fail to live according to his Will, does this bring misery to ourselves and others around us?

The Trials
of
Jesus

Chapter 31
Jesus Arrested and Questioned

Judas Iscariot, one of the twelve apostles helps the Jewish authorities to arrest Jesus.

Learning Outcome

- know how Jesus was arrested
- know the questions Caiaphas and Pilate asked Jesus
- know the details of Peter's denial of knowing Jesus.

Jesus Prays in Gethsemane

Then cometh Jesus with them unto a place called Gethsemane, and saith unto the disciples, sit ye here, while I go and pray yonder.

And he took with him Peter and the two sons of Zebedee and began to be sorrowful and very heavy.

Then saith he unto them, my soul is exceeding sorrowful, even unto death: tarry ye here, and watch with me.

And he went a little farther, and fell on his face, and prayed, saying, O my Father, if it be possible, let this cup pass from me: nevertheless, not as I will, but as thou wilt.

And there appeared an angel unto him from heaven, strengthening him.

And being in an agony he prayed more earnestly: and his sweat was as it were great drops of blood falling down to the ground.

And he cometh unto the disciples, and findeth them asleep, and saith unto Peter, What, could ye not watch with me one hour?

Watch and pray, that ye enter not into temptation: the spirit indeed is willing, but the flesh is weak.

He went away again the second time, and prayed, saying, O my Father, if this cup may not pass away from me, except I drink it, thy will be done.

And he came and found them asleep again: for their eyes were heavy.

And he left them, and went away again, and prayed the third time, saying the same words.

Then cometh he to his disciples, and saith unto them, Sleep on now, and take your rest: behold, the hour is at hand, and the Son of man is betrayed into the hands of sinners.

Rise, let us be going: behold, he is at hand that doth betray me. (Matthew 26: 36-46; Luke 22: 43-44 KJV)

The Arrest of Jesus

The Servant's Ear Healed (Miracle 34)

When Jesus had spoken these words, he went forth with his disciples over the brook Cedron, where was a garden, into the which he entered, and his disciples.

And Judas also, which betrayed him, knew the place: for Jesus ofttimes resorted thither with his disciples.

Judas then, having received a band of men and officers from the chief priests and Pharisees, cometh thither with lanterns and torches and weapons.
(John 18: 1-3 KJV)

Now he that betrayed him gave them a sign, saying, Whomsoever I shall kiss, that same is he: hold him fast.

And forthwith he came to Jesus, and said, Hail, master; and kissed him.

And Jesus said unto him, Friend, wherefore art thou come? Then came they, and laid hands on Jesus and took him.
(Matthew 26: 48-50 KJV)

Jesus, therefore, knowing all things that should come upon him, went forth, and said unto them, whom seek ye?

They answered him, Jesus of Nazareth. Jesus saith unto them, I am he. And Judas also, which betrayed him, stood with them.

As soon then as he had said unto them, I am he, they went backward, and fell to the ground.

Then asked he them again, whom seek ye? And they said, Jesus of Nazareth.

Jesus answered, I have told you that I am he: if therefore ye seek me, let these go their way:
(John 18: 4-8 KJV)

And one of them smote the servant of the high priest and cut off his right ear.

And Jesus answered and said, Suffer ye thus far. And he touched his ear and healed him.
(Luke: 22: 50-51 KJV)

Then said Jesus unto him, put up again thy sword into his place: for all they that take the sword shall perish with the sword.

Thinkest thou that I cannot now pray to my Father, and he shall presently give me more than twelve legions of angels?

But how then shall the scriptures be fulfilled, that thus it must be?

In that same hour said Jesus to the multitudes, are ye come out as against a thief with swords and staves for to take me? I sat daily with you teaching in the temple, and ye laid no hold on me.

But all this was done, that the scriptures of the prophets might be fulfilled. Then all the disciples forsook him and fled.
(Matthew 26: 52-56 KJV)

Jesus is Questioned by Caiaphas

And they that had laid hold on Jesus led him away to Caiaphas the high priest, where the scribes and the elders were assembled.

But Peter followed him afar off unto the high priest's palace, and went in, and sat with the servants, to see the end.

Now the chief priests, and elders, and all the council, sought false witness against Jesus, to put him to death;

But found none: yea, though many false witnesses came, yet found they none. At the last came two false witnesses,

And said, this fellow said, I am able to destroy the temple of God, and to build it in three days.

And the high priest arose, and said unto him, Answerest thou nothing? what is it which these witness against thee?

Jesus held his peace, And the high priest answered and said unto him, I adjure thee by the living God, that thou tell us whether thou be the Christ, the Son of God.

Jesus saith unto him, thou hast said: nevertheless I say unto you, Hereafter shall ye see the Son of man sitting on the right hand of power and coming in the clouds of heaven.

Then the high priest rent his clothes, saying, He hath spoken blasphemy; what further need have we of witnesses? behold, now ye have heard his blasphemy.

What think ye? They answered and said, He is guilty of death.

Then did they spit in his face, and buffeted him; and others smote him with the palms of their hands,

Saying, Prophesy unto us, thou Christ, who is he that smote thee? (Matthew 26: 57-68 KJV)

Peter Denies Jesus Three Times

Now Peter sat without in the palace: and a damsel came unto him, saying, Thou also wast with Jesus of Galilee.

But he denied before them all, saying, I know not what thou sayest.

And when he was gone out into the porch, another maid saw him, and said unto them that were there, this fellow was also with Jesus of Nazareth.

And again, he denied with an oath, I do not know the man.

And after a while came unto him, they that stood by, and said to Peter, Surely, thou also art one of them; for thy speech bewrayeth thee.

Then began he to curse and to swear, saying, I know not the man. And immediately the cock crew.

And Peter remembered the word of Jesus, which said unto him, Before the cock crow, thou shalt deny me thrice. And he went out and wept bitterly. (Matthew 26: 69-75 KJV)

Jesus is Taken to Pilate

And the whole multitude of them arose and led him unto Pilate.

And they began to accuse him, saying, we found this fellow perverting the nation, and forbidding to give tribute to Caesar, saying that he himself is Christ a King.

And Pilate asked him, saying, Art thou the King of the Jews? And he answered him and said, Thou sayest it.

Then said Pilate to the chief priests and to the people, I find no fault in this man.

And they were the more fierce, saying, He stirreth up the people, teaching throughout all Jewry, beginning from Galilee to this place.

When Pilate heard of Galilee, he asked whether the man were a Galilean.

And as soon as he knew that he belonged unto Herod's jurisdiction, he sent him to Herod, who himself also was at Jerusalem at that time. (Luke 23: 1-7 KJV)

Jesus is Questioned by Herod

And when Herod saw Jesus, he was exceeding glad: for he was desirous to see him of a long season, because he had heard many things of him; and he hoped to have seen some miracle done by him.

Then he questioned with him in many words; but he answered him nothing.

And the chief priests and scribes stood and vehemently accused him.

And Herod with his men of war set him at nought, and mocked him, and arrayed him in a gorgeous robe, and sent him again to Pilate.

And the same day Pilate and Herod were made friends together: for before they were at enmity between themselves.
(Luke 23: 8-12 KJV)

Jesus is Taken to Pilate for the Second Time

Pilate, when he had called together the chief priests and the rulers and the people,

Said unto them, Ye have brought this man unto me, as one that perverteth the people: and, behold, I, having examined him before you, have found no fault in this man touching those things whereof ye accuse him:

No, nor yet Herod: for I sent you to him; and, lo, nothing worthy of death is done unto him.

I will therefore chastise him and release him.

Now at that feast he released unto them one prisoner, whomsoever they desired.

And there was one named Barabbas, which lay bound with them that had made insurrection with him, who had committed murder in the insurrection.

And the multitude crying aloud began to desire him to do as he had ever done unto them.

But Pilate answered them, saying, Will ye that I release unto you the King of the Jews?

For he knew that the chief priests had delivered him for envy.

But the chief priests moved the people, that he should rather release Barabbas unto them.

And Pilate answered and said again unto them, what will ye then that I shall do unto him whom ye call the King of the Jews?

And they cried out again, Crucify him.

Then Pilate said unto them, Why, what evil hath he done? And they cried out the more exceedingly, Crucify him.

When he was set down on the judgment seat, his wife sent unto him, saying, have thou nothing to do with that just man: for I have suffered many things this day in a dream because of him.

When Pilate saw that he could prevail nothing, but that rather a tumult was made, he took water, and washed his hands before the multitude, saying, I am innocent of the blood of this just person: see ye to it.

Then answered all the people, and said, His blood be on us, and on our children.

Then released he Barabbas unto them: and when he had scourged Jesus, he delivered him to be crucified.
(Luke 23: 13-17; Mark 15: 6-14; Matthew 27: 19, 24 – 26 KJV)

Focus Questions

1	How were the soldiers able to identify who Jesus was before arresting him?	4	How many times did Peter deny not knowing Jesus?
2	Why did Pilate send Jesus to Herod?	5	Why did Pilate try to set Jesus free?
3	Why was Herod happy to meet Jesus?	6	Why couldn't Pilate set Jesus free?

Note:

It is comforting to know that even Jesus was not at ease with his imminent fate, despite knowing God's plan for him. When faced with crises in our lives, we should not be ashamed of our fears and doubts, and our instinct for self-preservation. However, what made Jesus an example to us is his willingness to sacrifice himself for the sake of others, something that was made possible by his faith in God's plan. In direct contrast are the actions of someone like Pilate, who realizes that what is happening is wrong but does not want to take a stand to stop the injustice. Did he think that he is innocent just because he did not personally order to take the life of Jesus by crucifying him on the cross? No doubt we can all identify with the dilemma Pilate faced, but we always have a choice when it comes to the decisions we finally make regarding truth.

Reflection

Every-one of us makes decisions that are both life-changing and inconsequential. God has given us a mind and capability to reason, but He always wants to guide us in our decision making, provided we seek his help. This way we will not make mistakes, and we can become more and more like Jesus

Chapter 32
Jesus Suffers and Dies for Us

Jesus is mocked, scourged and made to carry the cross before being crucified.

Learning Outcome

- know how Jesus was mocked and scourged.
- know the details of the events that happened when Jesus was carrying the cross to Calvary
- know the details of the events that happened while Jesus was on the cross.

Jesus is Mocked

Then the soldiers of the governor took Jesus into the common hall and gathered unto him the whole band of soldiers.

And they stripped him and put on him a scarlet robe.

And when they had platted a crown of thorns, they put it upon his head, and a reed in his right hand: and they bowed the knee before him, and mocked him, saying, Hail, King of the Jews!

And they spit upon him, and took the reed, and smote him on the head. (Mathew 27: 27-30 KJV)

Jesus Carries the Cross

And he bearing his cross went forth into a place called the place of a skull, which is called in the Hebrew Golgotha.

And as they came out, they found a man of Cyrene, Simon by name: him they compelled to bear his cross.

And there followed him a great company of people, and of women, which also bewailed and lamented him.

But Jesus turning unto them said, Daughters of Jerusalem, weep not for me, but weep for yourselves, and for your children.

For, behold, the days are coming, in the which they shall say, blessed are the barren, and the wombs that never bare, and the paps which never gave suck.

Then shall they begin to say to the mountains, fall on us; and to the hills, Cover us.

For if they do these things in a green tree, what shall be done in the dry? (John 19: 17; Matthew 27: 32; Luke 23: 27-31 KJV)

Jesus On the Cross

And there were also two others, malefactors, led with him to be put to death.

And when they were come to the place, which is called Calvary, there they crucified him, and the malefactors, one on the right hand, and the other on the left.

Then said Jesus, Father, forgive them; for they know not what they do. And they parted his raiment and cast lots.

And the people stood beholding. And the rulers also with them derided him, saying, He saved others; let him save himself, if he be Christ, the chosen of God.

And the soldiers also mocked him, coming to him, and offering him vinegar,

And saying, if thou be the king of the Jews, save thyself.

And a superscription also was written over him in letters of Greek, and Latin, and Hebrew, This Is the King of The Jews.

Then said the chief priests of the Jews to Pilate, write not, The King of the Jews; but that he said, I am King of the Jews.

Pilate answered, What I have written I have written.

And one of the malefactors which were hanged railed on him, saying, if thou be Christ, save thyself and us.

But the other answering rebuked him, saying, Dost not thou fear God, seeing thou art in the same condemnation?

And we indeed justly; for we receive the due reward of our deeds: but this man hath done nothing amiss.

And he said unto Jesus, Lord, remember me when thou comest into thy kingdom.

And Jesus said unto him, Verily I say unto thee, today shalt thou be with me in paradise.

Then the soldiers, when they had crucified Jesus, took his garments, and made four parts, to every soldier a part; and also his coat: now the coat was without seam, woven from the top throughout.

They said therefore among themselves, let us not rend it, but cast lots for it, whose it shall be: that the scripture might be fulfilled, which saith, They parted my raiment among them, and for my vesture they did cast lots. These things therefore the soldiers did.
(Luke 23: 32 - 43; John 19: 21-24)

Jesus Dies on the Cross

And it was about the sixth hour, and there was a darkness over all the earth until the ninth hour. And the sun was darkened, and the veil of the temple was rent in the midst.

Now there stood by the cross of Jesus his mother, and his mother's sister, Mary the wife of Cleophas, and Mary Magdalene.

When Jesus therefore saw his mother, and the disciple standing by, whom he loved, he saith unto his mother, Woman, behold thy son!

Then saith he to the disciple, Behold thy mother! And from that hour that disciple took her unto his own home.

After this, Jesus knowing that all things were now accomplished, that the scripture might be fulfilled, saith, I thirst.

Now there was set a vessel full of vinegar: and they filled a spunge with vinegar, and put it upon hyssop, and put it to his mouth.

When Jesus therefore had received the vinegar, he said, It is finished: and he bowed his head, and gave up the ghost.

And about the ninth hour Jesus cried with a loud voice, saying, Eli, Eli, lama sabachthani? that is to say, My God, my God, why hast thou forsaken me?

Some of them that stood there, when they heard that, said, This man calleth for Elias. The rest said, Let be, let us see whether Elias will come to save him.

Jesus, when he had cried again with a loud voice, yielded up the ghost. And, behold, the veil of the temple was rent in twain from the top to the bottom; and the earth did quake, and the rocks rent; And the graves were opened; and many bodies of the saints which slept arose,
(Luke 23: 44-45; John: 19: 25-30; Matthew 27: 45-47, 49 KJV)

Death of Judas

Then Judas, which had betrayed him, when he saw that he was condemned, repented himself, and brought again the thirty pieces of silver to the chief priests and elders,

Saying, I have sinned in that I have betrayed the innocent blood. And they said, what is that to us? see thou to that.

And he cast down the pieces of silver in the temple, and departed, and went and hanged himself.

And the chief priests took the silver pieces, and said, it is not lawful for to put them into the treasury, because it is the price of blood.

And they took counsel, and bought with them the potter's field, to bury strangers in. Wherefore that field was called, The field of blood, unto this day.

Then was fulfilled that which was spoken by Jeremy the prophet, saying, and they took the thirty pieces of silver, the price of him that was valued, whom they of the children of Israel did value; And gave them for the potter's field, as the Lord appointed me.
(Matthew 27: 3-10 KJV)

Focus Questions

1	How was Jesus mocked?	4	What did Jesus say to the criminal crucified on his right?
2	Summarize what happened when Jesus was on the cross.	5	State all what Jesus said before he breathed his last.
3	What did the criminal crucified on the left of Jesus say?	6	How did Judas end his life?

Note:

In the description of the events surrounding the crucifixion, there are several people that question why Jesus did not save himself if he had the power to do so. Everyone's natural instinct would be to do the same and, once again, this demonstrates the faith of Jesus in God and his plan. God wanted to redeem the world and Jesus was required to accept the suffering for this redemption. Equally interesting was Judas' fate – regretting for our unethical actions when it is too late is a very human trait. Regretting and asking God's forgiveness for our wrongs or failures would suffice instead of going to the extent of committing suicide like Judas did.

He committed suicide out of despair.

Reflection

Jesus loved us so much, that he gave up his life freely to teach us the right way to live. Wouldn't it be proper to surrender ourselves to God's call? The cross is the greatest sign we will ever have of perfect, loving obedience to the will of God.

The Triumph
of
Jesus

Chapter 33
Jesus Rises from Death

As he told publicly during his ministry, Jesus rose from death on the third day after the crucifixion.

Learning Outcome

- know what happened between the death of Jesus and his resurrection on the third day.

Events that Happened When Jesus Died

Now when the centurion, and they that were with him, watching Jesus, saw the earthquake, and those things that were done, they feared greatly, saying, truly this was the Son of God.

And all the people that came together to that sight, beholding the things which were done, smote their breasts, and returned.
(Matthew 27: 54; Luke 23: 48 KJV)

Jesus's Side is Pierced

The Jews, therefore, because it was the preparation, that the bodies should not remain upon the cross on the sabbath day, (for that sabbath day was an high day,) besought Pilate that their legs might be broken, and that they might be taken away.

Then came the soldiers, and brake the legs of the first, and of the other which was crucified with him.

But when they came to Jesus, and saw that he was dead already, they brake not his legs:

But one of the soldiers with a spear pierced his side, and forthwith came there out blood and water.

And he that saw it bare record, and his record is true: and he knoweth that he saith true, that ye might believe.

For these things were done, that the scripture should be fulfilled, A bone of him shall not be broken.

And again, another scripture saith, they shall look on him whom they pierced.
(John 19: 31-37 KJV)

The Burial of Jesus

When the even was come, there came a rich man of Arimathaea, named Joseph, who also himself was Jesus' disciple:

He went to Pilate and begged the body of Jesus.

Pilate marveled that He was already dead; and summoning the centurion, he asked him if He had been dead for some time. So, when he found out from the centurion, he granted the body to Joseph.

And Nicodemus, who at first came to Jesus by night, also came, bringing a mixture of myrrh and aloes, about a hundred pounds.

Then they took the body of Jesus and bound it in strips of linen with the spices, as the custom of the Jews is to bury.

Now in the place where He was crucified there was a garden, and in the garden a new tomb in which no one had yet been laid.

So there they laid Jesus, because of the Jews' Preparation Day, for the tomb was nearby.
(Matthew 27: 57-58; Mark 15: 44-45; John 19: 39-42 KJV)

The Guard at The Tomb

Now the next day, that followed the day of the preparation, the chief priests and Pharisees came together unto Pilate,

Saying, Sir, we remember that that deceiver said, while he was yet alive, after three days I will rise again.

Command therefore that the sepulchre be made sure until the third day, lest his disciples come by night, and steal him away, and say unto the people, He is risen from the dead: so, the last error shall be worse than the first.

Pilate said unto them, Ye have a watch: go your way, make it as sure as ye can.

So, they went, and made the sepulchre sure, sealing the stone, and setting a watch.
(Matthew 27: 62-66 KJV)

The Resurrection of Jesus

Now after the Sabbath, as the first day of the week began to dawn, Mary Magdalene and the other Mary came to see the tomb.

And behold, there was a great earthquake; for an angel of the Lord descended from heaven and came and rolled back the stone from the door and sat on it. His countenance was like lightning, and his clothing as white as snow.

And the guards shook for fear of him and became like dead men

And go quickly and tell his disciples that he is risen from the dead; and, behold, he goeth before you into Galilee; there shall ye see him: lo, I have told you.

And they departed quickly from the sepulchre with fear and great joy; and did run to bring his disciples word.
(Matthew 28: 1-4, 7-8 KJV)

Focus Questions

1	How did the nature react when Jesus died?	4	Who brought Jesus' body down from the cross?
2	Why were the legs of the criminals broken but not those of Jesus?	5	How did they bury Jesus' body?
3	How did they secure Jesus' tomb?	6	Who were the first to find out that Jesus had risen?

Note:

The resurrection of Jesus not only provides us with additional proof of the accuracy of the scriptures, but also gives us much needed reassurance about what lies ahead of us after this life. Regardless of the suffering we endure during our lives, believing in God will lead us to his side after our death where we will find eternal fulfilment.

Death of the physical body is only a 'ritual' to invoke our eternal happiness in the Kingdom of God. It is only our spiritual body that should be alive and well. For those of us who do not believe in life after death, how hard it must be to live life without fear of failing to achieve what is needed in this limited life span?

254

Reflection

Jesus rose from the dead, as foretold by the prophets, demonstrating our ability to transcend this earthly life. The resurrection of Jesus gives us the hope that we too will rise from the dead and enjoy eternal life with God.

Chapter 34
Appearances of Jesus And His
Ascension into Heaven

Jesus appears to disciples and others after his resurrection, makes Peter the head of his flock before ascending to heaven to return to his Father.

Learning Outcome

- know to whom Jesus appeared first after resurrection
- know what the chief priests and elders did to conceal the truth about Jesus's resurrection.
- know how Jesus appeared to the apostles
- know what happened on the way to Emmaus
- know the miracle Jesus performed after resurrection
- know how Jesus was taken up to heaven.

Mary Magdalene Informs Peter and John

The first day of the week cometh Mary Magdalene early, when it was yet dark, unto the sepulchre, and seeth the stone taken away from the sepulchre.

Then she runneth, and cometh to Simon Peter, and to the other disciple, whom Jesus loved, and saith unto them, they have taken away the Lord out of the sepulchre, and we know not where they have laid him.

Peter therefore went forth, and that other disciple, and came to the sepulchre.

So, they ran both together: and the other disciple did outrun Peter and came first to the sepulchre.

And he stooping down, and looking in, saw the linen clothes lying; yet went he not in.

Then cometh Simon Peter following him, and went into the sepulchre, and seeth the linen clothes lie,

And the napkin, that was about his head, not lying with the linen clothes, but wrapped together in a place by itself.

Then went in also that other disciple, which came first to the sepulchre, and he saw, and believed.

For as yet they knew not the scripture, that he must rise again from the dead.

Then the disciples went away again unto their own home. (John 20: 1-10 KJV)

Risen Jesus Appears to Mary Magdalene

But Mary stood without at the sepulchre weeping: and as she wept, she stooped down, and looked into the sepulchre,

And seeth two angels in white sitting, the one at the head, and the other at the feet, where the body of Jesus had lain.

And they say unto her, Woman, why weepest thou? She saith unto them, because they have taken away my Lord, and I know not where they have laid him.

And when she had thus said, she turned herself back, and saw Jesus standing, and knew not that it was Jesus.

Jesus saith unto her, Woman, why weepest thou? whom seekest thou? She, supposing him to be the gardener, saith unto him, Sir, if thou have borne him hence, tell me where thou hast laid him, and I will take him away.

Jesus saith unto her, Mary. She turned herself, and saith unto him, Rabboni; which is to say, Master.

Jesus saith unto her, touch me not; for I am not yet ascended to my Father: but go to my brethren, and say unto them, I ascend unto my Father, and your Father; and to my God, and your God.

Mary Magdalene came and told the disciples that she had seen the Lord, and that he had spoken these things unto her.
(John 20: 11 - 18 KJV)

Then the same day at evening, being the first day of the week, when the doors were shut where the disciples were assembled for fear of the Jews, came Jesus and stood in the midst, and saith unto them, Peace be unto you.

The Report of the Guard

And when they were assembled with the elders, and had taken counsel, they gave large money unto the soldiers,

Saying, say ye, His disciples came by night, and stole him away while we slept.

And if this come to the governor's ears, we will persuade him, and secure you.

So they took the money and did as they were taught: and this saying is commonly reported among the Jews until this day.
(Matthew 28: 12-15 KJV)

Jesus Walks with Two Disciples to Emmaus

And, behold, two of them went that same day to a village called Emmaus, which was from Jerusalem about threescore furlongs.

And they talked together of all these things which had happened.

And it came to pass, that, while they communed together and reasoned, Jesus himself drew near, and went with them.

But their eyes were holden that they should not know him.

And he said unto them, What manner of communications are these that ye have one to another, as ye walk, and are sad?

And the one of them, whose name was Cleopas, answering said unto him, Art thou only a stranger in Jerusalem, and hast not known the things which are come to pass there in these days?

And he said unto them, What things? And they said unto him, Concerning Jesus of Nazareth, which was a prophet mighty in deed and word before God and all the people:

And how the chief priests and our rulers delivered him to be condemned to death and have crucified him.

But we trusted that it had been he which should have redeemed Israel: and beside all this, today is the third day since these things were done.

Yea, and certain women also of our company made us astonished, which were early at the sepulchre;

And when they found not his body, they came, saying, that they had also seen a vision of angels, which said that he was alive.

And certain of them which were with us went to the sepulchre and found it even so as the women had said: but him they saw not.

Then he said unto them, O fools, and slow of heart to believe all that the prophets have spoken:

Ought not Christ to have suffered these things, and to enter into his glory?

And beginning at Moses and all the prophets, he expounded unto them in all the scriptures the things concerning himself.

And they drew nigh unto the village, whither they went and he made as though he would have gone further.

But they constrained him, saying, abide with us: for it is toward evening, and the day is far spent. And he went in to tarry with them.

And it came to pass, as he sat at meat with them, he took bread, and blessed it, and broke, and gave to them.

And their eyes were opened, and they knew him; and he vanished out of their sight.

And they said one to another, did not our heart burn within us, while he talked with us by the way, and while he opened to us the scriptures?

And they rose up the same hour, and returned to Jerusalem, and found the eleven gathered together, and them that were with them,

Saying, The Lord is risen indeed, and hath appeared to Simon.

And they told what things were done in the way, and how he was known of them in breaking of bread
(Luke 24:13-35 KJV)

Jesus Appears to His Disciples First Time

Then the same day at evening, being the first day of the week, when the doors were shut where the disciples were assembled for fear of the

Jews, came Jesus and stood in the midst, and saith unto them, Peace be unto you.

And when he had so said, he shewed unto them his hands and his side. Then were the disciples glad, when they saw the Lord.

Then said Jesus to them again, Peace be unto you: as my Father hath sent me, even so send I you.

And when he had said this, he breathed on them, and saith unto them, Receive ye the Holy Ghost:

Whosesoever sins ye remit, they are remitted unto them; and whose soever sins ye retain, they are retained.

But Thomas, one of the twelve, called Didymus, was not with them when Jesus came.
(John 20: 19-25 KJV)

The Doubting Thomas

And after eight days again his disciples were within, and Thomas with them: then came Jesus, the doors being shut, and stood in the midst, and said, Peace be unto you.

Then saith he to Thomas, reach hither thy finger, and behold my hands; and reach hither thy hand and thrust it into my side: and be not faithless but believing.

And Thomas answered and said unto him, My Lord and my God.

Jesus saith unto him, Thomas, because thou hast seen me, thou hast believed: blessed are they that have not seen, and yet have believed.
(John 20: 26-29 KJV)

Risen Jesus Eats with the Disciples

And while they yet believed not for joy, and wondered, he said unto them, Have ye here any meat?

And they gave him a piece of a broiled fish, and of an honeycomb.

And he took it and did eat before them.
(Luke 21:41-43 KJV)

Jesus Appears to His Disciples Again

The Draught of Fishes (Miracle 35)

There were together Simon Peter, and Thomas called Didymus, and Nathanael of Cana in Galilee, and the sons of Zebedee, and two other of his disciples.

Simon Peter saith unto them, I go a fishing. They say unto him, we also go with thee. They went forth and entered into a ship immediately; and that night they caught nothing.

But when the morning was now come, Jesus stood on the shore: but the disciples knew not that it was Jesus.

Then Jesus saith unto them, Children, have ye any meat? They answered him, No.

And he said unto them, Cast the net on the right side of the ship, and ye shall find. They cast therefore, and now they were not able to draw it for the multitude of fishes.

Therefore, that disciple whom Jesus loved saith unto Peter, It is the Lord. Now when Simon Peter heard that it was the Lord, he girt his fisher's coat unto him, (for he was naked,) and did cast himself into the sea.

And the other disciples came in a little ship; (for they were not far from land, but as it were two hundred cubits,) dragging the net with fishes.

As soon then as they were come to land, they saw a fire of coals there, and fish laid thereon, and bread.

Jesus saith unto them, bring of the fish which ye have now caught.

Simon Peter went up, and drew the net to land full of great fishes, an hundred and fifty and three: and for all there were so many, yet was not the net broken.

Jesus saith unto them, Come and dine. And none of the disciples durst ask him, who art thou? knowing that it was the Lord.

Jesus then cometh, and taketh bread, and giveth them, and fish likewise. (John 21: 2-13 KJV)

Jesus Instructs His Disciples

And Jesus came and spoke unto them, saying, All power is given unto me in heaven and in earth.

Go ye therefore, and teach all nations, baptizing them in the name of the Father, and of the Son, and of the Holy Ghost:

And when he had said this, he breathed on them, and saith unto them, Receive ye the Holy Ghost:

Whose soever sins ye remit, they are remitted unto them; and whose soever sins ye retain, they are retained.

Teach them to observe all things whatsoever I have commanded you: and, lo, I am with you always, even unto the end of the world. Amen. (Matthew 28: 18 John 20: 22-23 KJV)

Jesus Makes Peter the Head of His Flock

So, when they had dined, Jesus saith to Simon Peter, Simon, son of Jonas, lovest thou me more than these? He saith unto him, Yea, Lord; thou knowest that I love thee. He saith unto him, Feed my lambs.

He saith to him again the second time, Simon, son of Jonas, lovest thou me? He saith unto him, Yea, Lord; thou knowest that I love thee. He saith unto him, Feed my sheep.

He saith unto him the third time, Simon, son of Jonas, lovest thou me? Peter was grieved because he said unto him the third time, Lovest thou me? And he said unto him, Lord, thou knowest all things; thou knowest that I love thee. Jesus saith unto him, Feed my sheep.

Verily, verily, I say unto thee, when thou wast young, thou girdest thyself, and walkedst whither thou wouldest: but when thou shalt be old, thou shalt stretch forth thy hands, and another shall gird thee, and carry thee whither thou wouldest not.
(John 21: 15-18 KJV)

Jesus is Taken Up to Heaven

And, behold, I send the promise of my Father upon you: but tarry ye in the city of Jerusalem, until ye be endued with power from on high.

And he led them out as far as to Bethany, and he lifted up his hands, and blessed them.

And it came to pass, while he blessed them, he was parted from them, and carried up into heaven.
(Luke 24: 49-51 KJV)

Focus Questions

1	Who saw the risen Jesus first?	5	What instruction did Jesus give the apostles when he appeared to them?
2	How did the chief priests and the elders try to hide the truth about Jesus' resurrection?	6	What miracle did Jesus perform after his resurrection?
3	Who were the disciples who met Jesus on their way to Emmaus?]	7	What did Jesus tell Peter before his ascension into heaven?
4	Why is the apostle Thomas called 'doubting Thomas'?	8	How did Jesus ascend to heaven?

Note:

Many people believed in God's power after they saw proof of this in the miracles Jesus performed, and the resurrection of Jesus. Our challenge is to have the same belief without the obvious proof that was seen by those present at that time. Having said that, if we look carefully, many (if not all) of us will experience events in our lives that could be considered miracles. If we choose to open our eyes, our lives could be richer and more fulfilling than we can imagine.

Reflection

Jesus presented himself in person to many people after his resurrection. He reveals himself to us through his teachings, the scriptures and his creations, especially through the love and kindness of the people with whom we live, work and play.

Articles of Interest

The words of Jesus and The Future Generation

Jesus repeatedly mentioned His Kingdom in the future. By this He meant a new way of life, a new set of values, a new order, and commitments.

Sweeping changes are happening in the world every day and modern technology is facilitating this. However, Jesus Christ is the same in the past, in the present, and in the future."

What Jesus said and did as written in the four gospels is exactly what He is saying and doing now.

Non-Christians always considered Jesus as a prophet and admired his teachings, especially the importance of loving one's neighbors.

Hindus tend to believe Jesus to be a legitimate manifestation of the divine, and many Buddhists have no problem seeing Jesus as one of humanity's most enlightened people. Jesus' messages would provide a common ground for the urgently needed religious exchange of ideas.

It is hoped that through interbelief dialogue people would start loving their enemies and thirst for justice. By the grace of God, there will be fewer and fewer wars and less and less violence. Perhaps wars will begin to fade like slavery, prejudice and racism and that people will be able to say that the kingdom of God has finally come.

People will join God in joy. They will share God's pleasure in every little thing they do. They will join God in love. They will begin to love what God loves, and not love what God doesn't love. This includes pride, cruelty, fear, apathy, and every other bad thing.

The new way of life should include new ways of learning about Jesus. Parents appear to have no time or interest in teaching Jesus's words to their kids and less and less importance is being given to this in schools. Not all teachers practice what they preach and thus fail to set a good example. The children left on their own will have no way of learning about the words of Jesus. Thus, a new way of instilling Jesus's messages in the minds of the children becomes a necessity.

Although there are many evangelists, there is definite need for people who will excel at telling the Christian Story in a winsome, memorable, and engaging manner. They should appear in the traditional churches as well. We need people who can deal with the complexities of life and paint a vision of the Christian gospel in all its glory.

Miracles of Jesus in All Ages

A miracle is something for which there is no natural explanation. It is something impossible that happens through the intervention of a greater power, God. For example, we have heard a student exclaim "it's a miracle that I got a credit in math in the last test, I was not prepared at all" or you may have heard someone say "a stranger from nowhere came to my rescue when I was stranded the other day".

Jesus was known for working miracles when he was on earth. The gospels record several miracles performed by Jesus. He did not heal everyone or bring back to life every dead person. He only healed the ones who put trust in him. Sometimes he physically touched the person whom he healed. The miracles represent the power of God.

Jesus's birth into this world by the womb of a virgin is a miracle. God being born in human flesh is miraculous.

Christians believe that Jesus's death and miraculous resurrection paved the way for the release of the Holy Spirit into the world. As a result, God's power for doing miracles is available and is at work against the forces of darkness and evil, of death and suffering.

Does Jesus still perform miracles today? After all, we don't see Him physically walking in our midst - or do we? We hear people known to us saying that someone was healed or someone whose life has been transformed by a relationship with Jesus. This is the modern-day miracle of Jesus. Every one of us can be an eyewitness to a miracle of Jesus. Miracles happen every day, all day long. Like Mary at the wedding in Cana, you can ask Him, believing He will do what is best for you. Let a miracle of Jesus begin in your heart right now.

Jesus performs miracles every day and in every age. He performs them only if we seek him, trust in his power and ask him fervently. He performs them through people we may not expect. We also see today's followers of Jesus doing precisely what Jesus told His followers during his time on earth to do. In hospitals we witness doctors, nurses, custodial staff, spiritual staff—doing miraculous acts, with whatever they're given, to restore broken bodies.

There are also unbelievable modern-day miracles that are reported in newspapers every day. In all these Jesus' intervention can be felt by those that believe in his powers.

Guides to the Bible

The **Bible**, the book containing the word of God, consists of two parts. The first part, the Old Testament is a covenant between God and Israel constituting the basis of the Hebrew religion. It has several books by various authors and the books are grouped into 5 sections

5 sections of the old testament

- Law: Genesis, Exodus, Leviticus, Numbers, and Deuteronomy.
- History: Joshua, Judges, Ruth, 1&2 Samuel, 1&2 Kings, 1&2 Chronicles, Ezra, Nehemiah, and Esther.
- Poetry and Wisdom books: Job, Psalms, Proverbs, Ecclesiastes, Song of Songs.
- Major Prophets
- Minor Prophets

Genesis – The book of beginnings.

Exodus - How God delivered the Israelites and made them His special people.

Leviticus - Laws about worship in general and customs & ceremonies.

Numbers - The culmination of the story of Israel's exodus from oppression in Egypt and their journey to take possession of the land God promised their fathers.

Deuteronomy – Moses's restated God's commands originally given to the Israelites some forty years earlier in Exodus and Leviticus.

History - the history of the Israelites with 12 books from Joshua through Esther;

Wisdom books - the Wisdom books deal with good and evil in the world.

Job - discusses why God allows pain.

Psalms contain the praise songs of David and others.

Proverbs are the sayings of the wise.

Ecclesiastes deal with the purpose and value of human life.

Song of Songs - Song of Solomon

The major and minor prophets: The major prophets were Isaiah, Jeremiah, Lamentations, Ezekiel and Daniel. There were some minor prophets like Hosea, Joel and so on. These prophets give warning of the consequences of turning away from God.

The coming of Jesus as deliverer and Savior was prophesied throughout the Old Testament. The Bible is the basis of Abrahamic religions which are Judaism, Christianity and Islam.

The second part of the Bible is the New Testament. It consists of the following:

1. The Gospel or the Good News which narrates the life, teaching, death and resurrection of Jesus

2, The Epistles which are the Twenty-one letters written by various authors, and consists of Christian doctrine, counsel, instruction, and conflict resolution.

3.An Apocalypse, or the Book of Revelation, which contains prophetical symbology about the end times.

Christians believe that God had one plan for salvation that was revealed first to the Israelites and then to all peoples through Jesus Christ. The New Testament and Old Testament, then, tell one ongoing story of salvation.

Reading the Bible on a consistent basis is important. We can find direction for our life and learn how to best serve the Lord who gave His life for us.

There is no set method to read the Bible. It is up to the individual where to begin. It is sensible to start at the beginning, but some prefer to start with the New testament.

Whatever method you choose, always pray to God before starting to read a Bible passage to reveal Himself and speak to you through His Word. Ask yourself "what does the passage I read teach me about God, and how can I apply it to my life?"

Always approach the Bible with the intention of understanding the big picture.

It is not always easy to understand the Bible passages.

We must learn to gather and absorb the situation, actions, qualities, and ideas being conveyed by the letters and words. We must understand the meaning, importance, and implications of what God is stating by the letters and words.

New Testament
Crossword Puzzles

New Testament Crossword Puzzle 1

Across

2 King of Judea when Jesus was born
4 The festival Jesus attended every year with the parents when he was young
9 Young children should follow this attribute of Jesus with their parents
10 Herod's wife's name
11 the town where Jesus grew up

Down

1 Another name for Jesus
3 Birth place of Jesus
5 The way John the Baptist died
6 Father of John the Baptist
7 Mary conceived by the power of -------
8 Relationship of John to Jesus

Word Bank

God	Passover	Bethlehem	Christ
Herodias	Nazareth	Zacharias	beheaded
Obedience	Cousin	Herod	

New Testament Crossword Puzzle 2

Across

3 The city in Galilee where Jesus performed his first miracle

6 Where Jesus began preaching

8 Simon Peter's brother

9 A parable usually has a hidden -------------

11 Jesus spoke ------- times about his death to the apostles

Down

1 The apostle who replaced Judas Iscariot

2 Jesus called the teachers of law and Pharisees -------------

4 This was one of the three apostles who was with Jesus at the time of his transfiguration

5 The apostle of Jesus who was a tax collector

7 Violation of the laws of God is tantamount to separation from ------

10 When Jesus referred to "needle's eye" he was referring to a --------- in Jerusalem

Word Bank

Cana	Hypocrites	Mathew	Mathias
Andrew	Three	Message	God
James	Galilee	Gate	

New Testament Crossword Puzzle 3

Across

3 The name of the Apostle who was not present when Jesus appeared first to the Apostles after his resurrection

7 The High Priest who questioned Jesus

8 The number of silver coins for which Judas Iscariot agreed to betray Jesus

9 The number of times Jesus spoke to his apostles about his death

10 The venue of Jesus' Passover meal before his death

12 Judas committed suicide by ------------

13 The number of times Jesus fell while carrying the Cross

Down

1 The name of the rich man from Arimathea who asked for Jesus' body

2 The name of the village to which Jesus walked with two disciples after his resurrection

4 The name of the High priest's slave whose ear Peter cut with his sword

5 The name of the place where Jesus was crucified

6 The number of times Simon Peter denied not knowing Jesus

11 The Roman Governor who couldn't find any reason to condemn Jesus

Word Bank

Hanging	Thomas	Malchus	Pilate
Three	Three	Emmaus	Upperroom
Joseph	Thirty	Caiaphas	Calvary

Some Old Testament Stories

1. Creation - Adam & Eve

God created heaven and the earth and all creatures.

God then created a man named **Adam** and then a woman named **Eve.**

Garden of Eden is the biblical earthly paradise inhabited by the first man and woman.

Most Bible commentaries state that the site of the Garden of Eden was in the Middle East,

Adam and Eve disobeyed God by eating the forbidden fruit and were sent out of Eden.

Adam and Eve had two sons, first born called **Cain** and **Abel**, the second one.

Cain was a land farmer, Abel was a sheep famer.

Cain Killed Abel through jealousy that God liked Abel's offerings more than his.

More children were born to Adam and Eve and they spread all over the earth. Another son named **Seth** was born after Abel's murder.

Noah was a direct descendant of Adam and was the son of **Lamech** belonging to the eighth generation.

All people living during the time of Noah were evil in the eyes of God except Noah, his wife and sons **Shem, Ham and Japheth** and their wives.

God wanted to destroy all the evil ones and asked Noah to build a boat 45 feet x 450 feet x 75 feet.

He put Noah's family and a pair (male and female) each of all animals in the boat (Noah's ARK) and brought down a flood to kill all the evil ones.

After 40 days of flood, God let the people out of the boat, blessed them and made them to multiply. Although the rain stopped after 40 days, Noah was in the ark for a year!

A direct descendent of Shem, son of Terah and Amathlaah was Abraham (formerly, Abram). His nephew was Lot, son of Haran. Abraham's father was the chief minister of King Nimrod of Babylon

Abraham's first wife was **Sarah**.
Abraham became restless with the promise of God and had a child with **Hagar** his slave.
Sarah had one child, only in her old age, named **Isaac**.
Isaac married **Rebekha**.

Isaac had two sons hairy **Esau** and **Jacob.**

Islam originated from **Ishmael**, Abraham's son from Hagar
God didn't approve of Abraham having a son with Hagar.

2. Abraham – The Father of Many Nations

God tested Abraham by asking his son to be given as a sacrifice and he obeyed. However, he was saved, and a lamb was sacrificed in his place.

Nimrod, the king was greatly afraid of Abraham. He gave him many precious gifts, among them **Eliezer,** a member of the king's household, who became Abraham's trusted servant and friend.

Abraham went as far as the sacred **tree of Moreh** in **Shechem** where God promised to him that he will give that land to his family forever. Abraham built an alter for God there.

Abraham travelled to a hill country east of **Bethel** and built another alter for God.

Abraham had another wife, whose name was **Keturah**. She bore him six children: Zimran, Jokshan, Medan, Midian, Ishbak and Shuah.

Abraham died at the age of 175 years leaving all his belongings to his son Isaac.

3. Isaac and His Twin Sons Esau and Jacob

Abraham had a brother called **Nahor** who lived in a city in Northern Syria.

Nahor married **Milcah** and had a son called **Bethuel.**

Bethuel had a daughter called **Rebekha.**

Isaac married **Rebekha** with the help of Abraham's servant.

Isaac was 40 years when he married Rebekha. They lived in the town of **Beersheba.**

Isaac and Rebekha did not have children for twenty years.

The twins Esau and Jacob were then born.

The two children became two nations.

Esau was a **hunter** and Jacob was a **shepherd.**

Esau hated his brother Jacob.

Rebekha sent her son Jacob to **Haran** through fear that Esau might kill him.

On his way to Haran Jacob rests in a place and while sleeping had a dream.

In the dream God told him "I will give you and your family this land"

Nahor's grandson is **Laban.**

Laban had two daughters **Leah** and **Rachel.**

Jacob worked for 7 years for Laban before getting married to Rachel whom he loved.

Since the older daughter had to marry first, Jacob had to spend a week with Leah before marrying Rachel. He had to work for another seven years for Laban.

As directed by an angel in a dream, Jacob took his wives and went to Canaan to live near Isaac.

On his way he had to wrestle with a stranger. He won and his name was changed to **Israel.**

Esau with his four hundred men met Jacob on the way and became friendly.

Esau left for **Edom** and Jacob went to **Succoth.**

4. Jacob and His Family

The Jewish forefather was Jacob.

Jacob (Israel) had **12 sons**.

Each son and his family were called a tribe.

Israel was conquered under the leadership of Joshua, and each of the tribes was designated an individual Territory except Levi who was to serve in the Temple.

Israel's family became the **twelve tribes of Israel**. They were called Israelites.

Jacob's family lived in the promised land of Canaan.

The names of Jacob's sons are: **Reuben, Simeon, Levi, Judah, Dan, Naphtali, Gad, Asher, Issachar, Zebulun, Joseph and Benjamin.**

Joseph was the favorite son of Jacob. This made the other sons to hate Joseph.

There are many interesting stories of the 12 sons of Jacob.

Joseph used to have dreams the meanings of which he explained to the brothers. The brothers were afraid of Joseph when the dreams were explained.

The brothers planned and threw him in a dry well out in the desert. Later they took him out and **sold him to the Ishmaelites for twenty pieces of silver** who took him to **Egypt.**

Joseph's fancy coat was dipped in goat's blood and the brothers gave it to their father Jacob saying that Joseph had been eaten by a wild animal.

5. Joseph in Egypt

Ishmaelites took Joseph to Egypt and sold him to the king's official **Potiphar**.

Potiphar realized that Joseph was being helped by God and made him his personal assistant.

Potiphar left all responsibilities to Joseph.

Potiphar's wife tried to seduce Joseph and when he resisted, she made false accusation and made Potiphar to put Joseph in prison.

Joseph interpreted fellow prisoner's dreams and they became true.

The King also had dreams and Joseph not only interpreted them but also warned him of the impending famine for seven years.

Joseph advised the king to appoint someone wise to store away one fifth of the harvest in the good years.

The King appointed Joseph himself for this job and made him the governor of Egypt.

Joseph was 30 years old when he became the governor. Later he succeeded as King.

When the famine came, the king sent the people of Egypt to buy grains from Joseph. Even people from other countries went to Egypt to get grains.

Ten of Joseph's brothers also went to Egypt to buy grains. They did not recognize Joseph. They told Joseph that they were from a family of 12 brothers, their youngest brother **Benjamin** is with their father Jacob in Canaan and that the other brother is dead.

Joseph remembered a dream he had and told them that they were spies. He said that he will trust them only if one of them stayed in Jail and the others went back and brought Benjamin to him. **Simeon** was left behind, and others went back to Canaan.

Jacob was very reluctant to send Benjamin to Egypt.

Reuben promised that he will bring back Benjamin and told Jacob that if he doesn't, Jacob could kill his (Reuben's) two sons.

Famine got worse in Canaan and Jacob agreed to send Benjamin.

Joseph's brothers went to Egypt again with gifts for Joseph.

Joseph was very excited to see his beloved brother Benjamin.

When the time came for Joseph's brothers to return to Canaan, Joseph told the servants to fill the brother's sacks with as much grain as possible and also put their money in each one's sack. He also asked them to put his silver cup in Benjamin's sack.

After the brothers left, Joseph sent his servants to follow them and accuse them of stealing his silver cup.

When they started searching, they found it in Benjamin's sack. The brothers had to go back to Joseph.

Joseph said that only the one who stole his cup will stay with him as his slave. The rest, he said, were free to go back to Canaan.

Judah pleaded with Joseph to let Benjamin go saying that their father had two sons from his favorite wife and that one is dead and the other is Benjamin.

He begged that Benjamin be allowed to go and that he will remain in his place as slave as he had promised the father that he would bring him home safely. He told Joseph that losing Benjamin would be more than the father could bear.

Finally, Joseph breaks down in tears and reveals his identity. Eventually, Jacob and Joseph's brothers settled in **Goshen.**

Joseph married **Asenath** and had two sons, **Ephraim** and **Manesseh.**

6. Moses

After Joseph died, an evil king **Pharaoh** ruled Egypt. Pharaoh made slaves of people and made them work hard.

He mistreated the Israelites in Egypt.

If a Hebrew woman gave birth to a boy, Pharaoh wanted him killed by throwing in the Nile River.

A Hebrew man from the Levi Tribe married a woman from the same tribe and they had a baby boy Called **Moses**.

Moses' mother kept the baby hidden for three months but could not keep him safe anymore. So she put him in a basket made of cane and placed the basket along the edge of the Nile river. Moses' older sister Miriam saw this happening.

When one of the king's daughters went to bathe in the river, she saw a crying baby in the basket and felt sorry. Miriam went to the princess and asked whether she could get a Hebrew woman to look after the baby. And the princess said "yes". Miriam brought her mother and princess told her to take care of the child and that she will pay her for that.

After Moses grew up, one day he saw an Egyptian beating a Hebrew man. He killed that Egyptian and hid his body in the sand.

Another day he saw two Hebrews fighting. He went and asked why they were fighting and one of them asked who put you in charge of us? "Do you want to kill us the way you killed the Egyptian?"

The king came to know of the killing by Moses and wanted to kill him. Moses quickly escaped to the land of **Midian**.

There was a priest called **Jethro in** Midian. He had seven daughters.

When the seven girls went to water the father's sheep and goats some shepherds tried to intimidate them, and Moses was there to rescue them and water the animals for them.

Moses stayed with Jethro and later married one of the daughters called **Zipporah.**

One day when Moses was looking after the animals, he decided to take them across the desert to **Sinai,** the Holy Mountain. Suddenly he saw a bush in front on fire but not burning!

He went near the bush to see what was happening, the Lord called him by name and Moses answered **"Here I am."** The voice said "Don't come any closer, take off your sandals, the ground you are standing is holy, I am the God your ancestors Abraham, Isaac and Jacob worshiped"

Moses was afraid and was hiding his face. God continued "I have seen how my people are suffering as slaves in Egypt, I have heard them beg me to save them, I am here to rescue them. **"You go to the king. I am sending you to lead the people out of his country."**

To prove to leaders of Israel that he was sent by God whose name is **"I am"**, he was commanded to do three things to make them believe

1. Throw the walking stick to the ground, it will turn into a snake. Pick it up by the tail and it will turn back into the stick.
2. Put the hand into the shirt, it will turn white as snow like someone with leprosy. Take it out of the shirt and it will return to normal.
3. Take some water from the Nile River and pour it on the ground. It will turn into blood.

7. Moses and Aaron

Moses had a brother called **Aaron** who was three years older than Moses. Both were the children of Jacob's third son Levi.

Aaron married **Elisheba** and had four sons.
Moses told God that he was not a good speaker and that the king may not listen to him.

So, God said that he will send Aaron who is a good speaker to go with him. He sent Aaron to meet Moses at the Mount Sinai.

Moses told Aaron about the miracles God has given power to perform. He performed these miracles in front of the people of Israel and they believed that they were sent by God.

Moses and Aaron went to the king and told him that God wants his people to be freed to go into the desert. But the king refused saying why he should obey God.

Moses and Aaron did whatever God commanded like turning the river Nile into blood, turning dust into a gnat, sending swarms of flies and so on. to make the king change his mind. The Egyptian magicians tried their secret tricks but failed. The king was still stubborn and would not let the Israelites go.

The Lord finally covered Egypt with darkness for three days. He sent word to the king through Moses that he was going to go through the land of Egypt and kill the first-born son in every Egyptian family and also the first-born male of every animal. When this happened, the king sent for Moses and Aaron and told them "Get your people out of my country and leave us alone".

After leaving Egypt the people of Israel went with Moses and set up camp at the foot of Mount Sinai. Moses went up the Mountain and God spoke to him face to face. On the morning of the third day everyone stood at the foot of the mountain that was covered with smoke. God came down and told them "I am the Lord your God who brought you out of slavery in Egypt" He then gave them TEN commandments to follow.

The Lord told Moses to choose a leader from each tribe and send them into Canaan to explore the land he was giving them.

Moses gave strict instructions to the people to obey the commands the Lord has given them and wordship him.

Moses died later in Moab. He was 120 years old when he died.

After Moses died Moses' assistant **Joshua** was asked by the Lord to lead Israel across the Jordan River into the land he was giving them.

Old Testament
Crossword Puzzles

Old Testament Crossword Puzzle - 1

Across

2. Descendent of Shem chosen by God
3. This person was asked to build the Ark
6. Number of male children for Noah
8. ------------made Cain to kill Abel
10. Garden where Adam and Eve started life
12. The first man God created
13. Isaac's wife

Down

1. Wife of Abraham
4. Name of Adam and Eve's second son
5. The promised son of Abraham
7. Abraham's Nephew
9. Name of the oldest son of Noah
11. The second of the twins of Rebekha

Word Bank

Adam	Isaac	Jacob	Shem
Three	Abraham	Abel	
Noah	Lot	Sarah	
Eden	Jealousy	Rebekha	

Old Testament Crossword Puzzle - 2

Across

1. Name of the sacred tree where Abraham was promised the land by God
4. Name of Lot's father
5. Abraham's former name
7. Place where Abraham's father lived
10. God promised to Abraham that he will make him the father of many --------
11. Abraham left all his belongings when dying, to this son
12. Number of children for Haran

Down

2. Abraham's mother's name
3. Which place did Abraham go to at the age of 75?
6. Abraham's trusted friend
8. God stopped the building of Tower --------------
9. Name of the King during Abraham's time

Word Bank

Three	Amathlaah	Abram	Babel
Babylon	Nations	Haran	Canaan
Moreh	Isaac	Nimrod	Eliezer

Old Testament Crossword Puzzle - 3

Across
2. Nahor's son
3. The place Jacob settled down
7. Place where Isaac lived with Rebekha
10. Nahor's wife
12. Place to where Rebekha sent her son Jacob through fear of Esau

Down
1. Esau was a ---------------
4. Nahor's grandson
5. Isaac's age when he married
6. Isaac's wife
8. The place Esau settled down
9. The new name given to Jacob
11. Laban's oldest daughter

Word Bank
Rebekha	Beersheba	Hunter	Edom
Israel	Forty	Leah	Laban
Haran	Succoth	Bethuel	Milcah

Old Testament Crossword Puzzle - 4

Across

3. Number of sons for Jacob
7. The favourite son of jacob
8. Joseph was famous for interpreting ------------
10. The age at which Joseph became the governor of Egypt
11. Whom did Ishmaelites sell Joseph to

Down

1. The name of the last son of Jacob
2. The place where Jacob and Joseph's brothers finally settled in.
4. The place where Jacob's family lived.
5. The reason why Joseph's brothers hated him.
6. Joseph's wife's name
9. The oldest son of Joseph

Word Bank

Ephraim	Benjamin	Asenath	Jealousy
Joseph	Dreams	Thirty	Twelve
Canaan	Goshen	Portiphar	

Old Testament Crossword Puzzle - 5

Across
2. The land to which Moses escape to when he was wanted for murder
6. The name of the mountain where God gave the Ten Commandments to Israelites
10. ----------succeeded Moses to lead Israel
11. Aaron's wife

Down
1. The name of Moses' oldest sister
3. The king of Egypt who succeeded Joseph
4. The name of the priest with whom Moses stayed
5. Moses' wife
7. Aaron was good at ----------------
8. Moses' brother
9. Place where Moses died

Word Bank
Midian	Aaron	Pharaoh	Joshua
Zipporah	Miriam	Moab	Jethro
Sinai	Speaking	Elisheba	

305

Appendix

Notes on Some Names and Places in This Book

NAME	NOTES
Barabbas	Barabbas was a robber and murderer who had been arrested by the Romans and was in prison awaiting execution at the time of the trial of Jesus. A Passover custom in Jerusalem allowed Pilate, the governor of Judaea, to commute one prisoner's death sentence by popular acclaim. The crowd wanted Jesus to be crucified in the place of Barabbas. Barabbas was the only man in the world who could say that Jesus took his physical place.
Bartimaeus	Blind Bartimaeus, was the son of Timaeus. He was a begger in Jericho. He called out to Jesus when he was passing his way saying 'Son of David have mercy on me.' Jesus healed him of his blindness.
Caiaphas	The son in law of the famous High Priest Annas. He became the High Priest after Annas. Caiaphas is the one who first questioned Jesus after his arrest.
Elizabeth	Elizabeth was the wife of Zechariah, a priest in Jerusalem. She was Mary's cousin and was the mother of John the Baptist.
Herod Antipas	Antipas was the son of the Jewish King Herod the great. He was appointed tetrarch of Galilee and Peraea. He is best known for his role in the events that led to the executions of John the Baptist and Jesus of Nazareth.
Herod Archelaus	Archelaus was the brother of Herod Antipas. Joseph feared Archelaus and took his family to Nazareth instead of settling in Bethlehem

307

NAME	NOTES
Herod the great	The Herod family was the ruling dynasty in Israel at the time of Jesus Herod the great was the son of Antipater. He is the one who tried to have the infant Jesus killed:
Jairus	Jairus was a ruler of the synagogue at Capernaum, whose only daughter Jesus restored to life
James 'the less'	James is the son of Cleopas (or Alpheus) and one of the twelve apostles of Jesus. Cleopas is the brother of Joseph (foster father of Jesus).
John (the beloved disciple of Jesus)	John leaned on the breast of Jesus at the last supper, stood with the Mother of Jesus at the foot of the cross, Jesus told him from the cross that Mary will be his mother, ran with Peter to the tomb after Mary Magdalen told them it was empty, the first to believe that Jesus had risen on the basis of the "sign" of the headpiece rolled, and the first to recognize Jesus on the shore of the sea of Galilee.
John the Baptist	John the Baptist was the son of Zecchariah, a priest of the Temple in Jerusalem, and Elizabeth, a kinswoman of Mary, the mother of Jesus. He was born 6 months before Jesus. He was born without original sin. He was beheaded on the instruction of King Herod.
Joseph of Arimathea	Joseph of Arimathea was not one of the original 12 apostles, but he was a disciple of Jesus and was an important man in his own right.
Joseph	Joseph was a carpenter. He was the spouse of the Blessed Virgin Mary and foster father of Jesus. He was the cousin of Zecchariah. It is believed that he died before the passion and death of Jesus.
Lazarus	Lazarus was the brother of Martha and Mary of Bethania; all three were beloved friends of Jesus. At the request of the two sisters Jesus raised Lazarus from the dead.

NAME	NOTES
Mary Cleopas	Wife of Cleopas (Alpe). She stood at the foot of the cross together with Mary the mother of Jesus and Mary of Magdala. She was that 'other Mary' who was present with Mary of Magdala at the burial of Jesus. She was also the first witness of the resurrection of Jesus.
Mary Magdalene	Mary Magdalene, a repentant sinner, came from a town called Magdala, 120 miles north of Jerusalem. She was the sister of Lazarus and Martha and the one who anointed Jesus at Simon's house. She was at the foot of the cross when Jesus died. She discovered the empty tomb of Jesus and was the first witness to his resurrection.
Nicodemus	Nicodemus was a ruler of the Jews of the group called the Pharisees. He believed that Jesus was truly a teacher sent from God. He was the one who was told by Jesus that if a person wanted to see the kingdom of God, he must be born again. Nicodemus was with Joseph of Arimathea when Jesus was buried.
Peter-'the rock'	Peter was from Bethsaida but lived in Capernaum. He was a fisherman, one of the first disciples of Jesus and one of his 12 apostles. Peter was introduced to Jesus by his brother Andrew. He was assigned a leadership role of the church by Jesus. He was the first pope and he died in Rome as a martyr.
Salome	Salome was the wife of Zebedee and the mother of the apostles James and John. She is the one who requested Jesus to keep one son on the right and the other son on the left in the Kingdom of God. She is one of those women who served Jesus.
Simon	Simon is a Pharisee from Bethany. He hosted a meal for Jesus during the course of which a woman anointed Jesus. He was cured of leprosy before.

NAME	NOTES
Simon of Cyrene	Simon was the father of Alexander and Rufus. He was forced to carry the cross for some time for Jesus by the Roman soldiers.
Zacchaeus	A rich, short man from Jericho. The Chief of the Publicans and a tax collector. He climbed a sycamore tree (a shade tree) to get a glimpse of Jesus when Jesus said to him 'Zacchaeus, you come down, for I'm coming to your house this day.'
Zechariah	Zechariah was a priest during the reign of King Herod the Great, and husband of Elizabeth, and the father of John the Baptist. He is also the cousin brother of Mary, the mother of Jesus.

PLACES	NOTES
Bethany	Bethany is the home of Mary, Martha and Lazarus, as well as that of Simon the Leper. Its exact location is unclear.
Bethlehem	Bethlehem is a town in Judaea about 6 miles from Jerusalem and sixty-six miles from Nazareth. This is where Jesus was born.
Bethsaida	Bethsaida is the birthplace of the apostles Peter, Andrew and Philip. This is where Jesus performed several miracles
Calvary	Calvary is the English equivalent of 'Golgotha', a skull shaped mountainous place used for public execution in Jerusalem.
Cana	Cana is a town in Galilee where Jesus attended a wedding and performed his first miracle, changing water into wine at the request of his mother.

PLACES	NOTES
Capernaum	Capernaum was a large Galilean fishing village and a busy trading center. It stood on the Northwestern shore of the Sea of Galilee, 4 km from the Jordan River. There was a synagogue for Jews here where Jesus frequently taught. Capernaum is also where Peter lived and Jesus healed his mother-in-law.
Emmaus	Emmaus is a village located about 8 miles from Jerusalem in Judaea.
Gethsemane	Gethsemane was the garden where Jesus and his disciples retreated to pray after the Last Supper. It was also where Jesus was betrayed by the disciple Judas Iscariot.
Jericho	Jericho is a town nine miles north of the Dead Sea. This is where Jesus healed the blind Bartimaeus.
Jerusalem	Jerusalem is the capital city of Judaea. It is the holiest city in Judaism and the spiritual center of the Jewish people. Jesus paid his first visit to Jerusalem in the arms of his mother when he was a month old. It was 12 years later he went there again. Finally, he did his triumphant entry into this city and was killed there.
Judaea	Judaea is situated south of Samaria. Its capital city is Jerusalem.
Naim	Naim is a city in Galilee where Jesus raised to life a widow's son.
Nazareth	Nazareth is the capital and largest city in the Northern District of Israel. This is where Jesus grew up. It is situated about 60 miles from Jerusalem.
Samaria	Samaria is situated South of Galilee and North of Judaea.
Sychar	Sychar is a town in Samaria, where Jesus spoke with a Samaritan woman who had come to a well - Jacob's well - to draw water.

The Family Tree

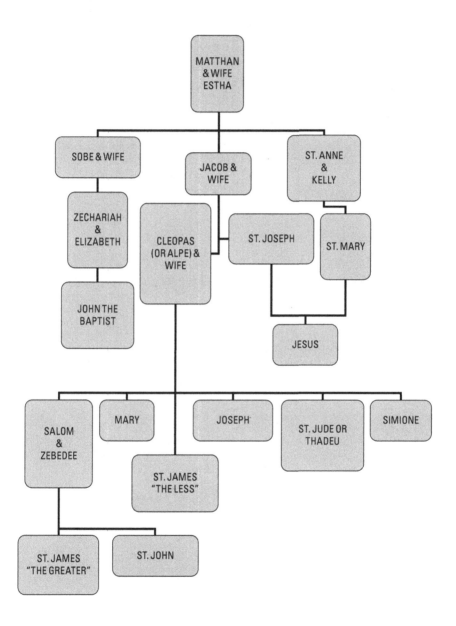

Printed in the United States
By Bookmasters